36 & GABBA

The Story of India's Greatest Cricketing Heist

YASHASWEE RAMAN

INDIA • SINGAPORE • MALAYSIA

ISBN 979-8-89233-475-4

Contents

Preface

Covid 19

2020 was thought to be a year for the sports fan. Euro's in the month of June, the Olympics in the month of July, and then the T20 World Cup in Australia in the month of October, which would have been followed by the Border Gavaskar Trophy in the months of December and January.

Being a sports fan, I told myself this year I would cover as many matches as possible,

But god had different plans, the universe was planning for people to get hurt. For people who had caused harm to nature, it was time for nature to take its redemption. A certain virus from Wuhan had gone berserk and it was in full plan to restrict humans in the four walls which the civilized animal had created for himself.

17th March 2020:

I was in the final semester of my Graduation at Ranchi. All excited for farewell and batch photography, knowing in hindsight that there is a virus that is causing chaos and we all might be locked in our rooms very soon.

It did turn out to be true as my college asked all of the students to vacate the hostels and go back home on an immediate basis. Didn't know my college life was going to end on such a bad note, but as they say " It is what it is". There is very little you could do and at a time when the world was looking to survive, I also decided to survive.

Least I knew I wouldn't meet my classmates again but knew one thing for sure life was not going to be the same and we were in for something special. The boy in me didn't know that he would go on to write two books.

21st March 2020:

Prime Minister Modi comes to the forefront and addresses the country. The whole nation was waiting in anticipation as to what would happen. Not to anybody's surprise a countrywide lockdown was announced, everything was shut. Only essential utilities were to be open that is grocery stores, banks, and hospitals. etc.

To be honest, at first, I thought this was going to be fun but honestly being away from the family and also being away from cricket was going to be hard. It was not going to be an easy task for most of us especially me.

Day 1 passed, and Day 2 passed all in anticipation that things would get under control and the number of covid positive cases would subside every day in and day out but nothing happened as such. With every passing day, the number of cases increased which also led to the increase in the anxiety of the people around.

IPL, which was supposed to happen in the same month, was postponed, people like me who had nothing to the were watching cricket and sports highlights to remove stress and anxiety.

Nothing better than test cricket helped me in that period, it was just watching classic five-day test matches in loop starting from Kolkata 2001 to Perth 2008 and Adelaide 2014, and so on.

With the number of COVID cases increasing worldwide, many people were afraid whether the T20 World Cup and the following tour of Australia would be conducted.

To everyone's fears, the T20 World Cup was cancelled and delayed which was to be played in Australia in 2022 where the Three Lions became the world champions.

The tour to Australia was confirmed and the Australian government was in readiness to host the Indians for the series. There were two reasons for this particular decision, One was to bring the smiles back onto the face of the fans, and the second which according to me was an important aspect was to stabilise the Australian economy. The Indian fans coming to the stadium wouldn't have only helped the morale of the cricketers but would also bring in different types of funds into the system.

Indian players after two months of toiling hard in the United Arab Emirates for the Indian Premier League were all set to tour Australia for a big fat 50-day tour to Australia. The tour consisted of 3 ODI's, 3 T20I's, and 4 Test Matches. The test series was going to be very important for India as it was going to fix a spot for India in the finals of the World Test Championship which was to be held in June 2021.

It wasn't going to be easy for the Indian team as the tour was being played during COVID times, quarantine and bio-bubble were a thing of the present The biggest roadblock for the Indian team was going to be the bio-bubble in which the players and support staffs were staying. To say the least, people thought it was going to be easy to stay in a bio bubble and do all the quarantine protocols but if you keep a certain person in one place, locked for a long period, the person will feel sick, which will create physical as well as mental issues for the player.

The Indian team had already stayed in the bio bubble during the IPL and they were accompanied by a few Aussie cricketers as well who were representing the various franchises in the IPL.

Bio bubble and the hostile Aussie cricketers and crowd were going to be crucial in this tour. Indian team on the other hand had already faced a few injury concerns as Vice-Captain Rohit Sharma and Star Indian bowler Ishant Sharma were ruled out of the series. Rohit who was ruled out off the limited-overs leg was supposed to make a comeback into the Indian team for the third test which was going to be played at Sydney.

Also, the Indian captain Virat Kohli had already informed the board that he wouldn't be a part of the team after the first test as he and his wife Anushka Sharma were expecting their first child in the month of January.

With already three big exclusions, it was time for the Indian team to step up big time to perform well and leave a mark.

Schedule:

ODI Series:

1st Match: 27th November, 2020 – Sydney Cricket Ground

2nd Match: 29th November, 2020- Sydney Cricket Ground

3rd Match: 2nd December, 2020- Manuka Oval

T20 Series:

1st T20I: 4th December, 2020- Manuka Oval

2nd T20I: 6th December, 2020- Sydney Cricket Ground

3rd T20I: 8th December, 2020- Sydney Cricket Ground

Test Series:

1st Test- 17th December- 21st December, 2020- Adelaide Oval

2nd Test- 26th December- 30th December, 2020- Melbourne Cricket Ground

3rd Test- 7th January- 11th January, 2021- Sydney Cricket Ground

4th Test- 15th January- 19th January, 2021- Gabba

Acknowledgment

There was a dream; There were people who supported the dream. I have always believed that my success is not my success alone, but the success of people who have supported and trusted me in all my dreams.

When I published my first book, my parents were ecstatic and I can't explain how happy they were, just after the release of the book, we had taken a trip to Nepal and had gone to the Pashupatinath Temple, where in front of God my mother had taken an oath saying this boy now has to write 11 books and this was just the beginning.

36 & Gabba wouldn't have been published without the believe and the faith my parents had on me, the love and affection and the amount of liberty they have given me is the reason why this book is here today.

Another person who needs to be mentioned is my sister, Sanjana. She has not only listened to my tantrums regarding my writer's block, but always pushed me to write 100-200 words when I was down and didn't wish to complete the book.

I will take this opportunity to thank my friends and mentors from the sporting circuit who supported and instilled confidence in me to write this book. I want to thank Venugopal Rajagopalan, Mahesh Kutty, Sidharth Gulati, Bhash Mankad, Suvajit Mustafi, Rajit Divetia, Vanshaj Singh, Anand Samat, Prasham Pratap and Dhruv Chhabra for their constant support and for helping me with a lot of information and knowledge, which enabled me to get better.

I also thank my friends like to name a few of them who had always been there for me no matter what, Swati Suman, Rishabh Mishra, Goutam Choudhury, Varad Terdal, Soumya Kakkar, Minnie Jaiswal, Shashank Suman, Sai Krishna Patra, and Akhil Radhakrishnan Kavya Kabra for their support and also for handling me no matter what.

Lastly, to the energy of Cricket that protected me and kept my love for the sport pure.

ODI Series

India's tour to Australia was all set to begin with the three-match ODI series. The ODI series was being played between two powerhouses of white ball cricket. Two teams who have played a lot of white-ball cricket with each other. India and Australia both knew the strengths and weaknesses of each other.

On one hand, the Indian team had a brilliant set of players but were missing Hitman, Rohit Sharma and with Mahendra Singh Dhoni announcing his retirement and Rishabh Pant being dropped from the team there was added responsibility on KL Rahul to control and stabilize the middle order and keep the wickets. KL Rahul was also named the vice-captain for the white ball series.

Hardik Pandya was also set to make a comeback into the Indian team but there were question marks raised whether Hardik would ball or not as the star Indian All-rounder hadn't bowled an over in the IPL for Mumbai Indians.

Australia on the other hand was playing in their home conditions and knew how to tackle the Indians, the biggest disadvantage for India was going to be the bio bubble fatigue that they had suffered from playing in the IPL.

Being a cricketer during the COVID times was difficult, from bio bubbles to daily rapid antigen testing and RTPCR Testing, and wearing Biohazard jackets while traveling was going to be difficult for the cricketers. Most importantly staying away from families was going to be tough for many cricketers.

Indian Squad for the ODI Series:

Virat Kohli, KL Rahul, Shikhar Dhawan, Shubman Gill, Shreyas Iyer, Manish Pandey, Mayank Agarwal, Hardik Pandya, Ravindra Jadeja, Sanju Samson, Yuzvendra Chahal, Kuldeep Yadav, Jasprit Bumrah, Mohammed Shami, Navdeep Saini, Shardul Thakur, T Natrajan.

While seeing the squad people and experts had made a sense that the Indian team was well sorted in their batting even though the team was without their star opener Rohit Sharma.

But more than the Indian team playing the game there were emotions of a billion people who were going to cheer for their team and wanted India to do extremely well. India was finally going to play an international game after 8 months.

The coronavirus had already taken away the Ranji trophy, as the coveted Domestic competition was canceled for the first time in 80 years.

The Indian team had a task on hand to help the Indians get over the suffering of the deadly virus, the cases were increasing at rates of knots and the signs of the virus spreading and causing havoc were ominous. We as fans just hoped for an Indian victory and a victory that would deviate the minds of the fans from the virus and bring happiness during the gloomy and bad times.

If I have to tell my personal experience, it wasn't a good time for me as well. I had enrolled myself into an MBA from TAPMI, but it was online, so I was sitting in Doha and attending my classes, but for me, the greatest issue was my sister's health. Sanjana was suffering from a severe case of Sciatica which needed a surgical intervention and the surgery was due on the 29th of November. The day when the second ODI was to be played.

With COVID around and life being hit with uncertainties people were finding their solace in the game. A game that would bring peace to the country and a lot of fans in the nation. Honestly, I was expecting a cracker jacker of a game, but deep down I knew it would be a difficult task for the Indian to regroup and focus on winning the ODI leg of the series and start the big 50-day tour on a good note.

1st ODI

27th November, 2020- Sydney Cricket Ground

The stage was all set at the historic Sydney Cricket Ground, International cricket was returning, and cricket was returning Down Under, and more than that the Indian cricket team was coming back. The Indian team donning their retro dark blue jersey from 1992, were all set to take center stage.

Covid had disrupted cricket all over the globe and now once International cricket was back, cricket was in no mood to surrender. The idea was simple to show the world what cricket could do and how well it could be used as a healer in a difficult period.

It was a bright sunny day in Sydney, Virat Kohli was leading India into this big series knowing and remembering his love affair with the country and how he could continue his form and get the elusive century that he was waiting for in 2020.

The whole world knew if there was one place where King Kohli would perform it would always be Australia, the Australian crowd, Australian sledging, and the Australian players boosted the Indian captain's form and performance.

Australian captain Aaron Finch won the toss and elected to bat first. The Indian team was going with a conventional team. Mayank Agarwal was handed the ODI cap and was making his debut for the Indian team in white ball cricket.

KL Rahul was pushed down the order as he was asked to keep and also keep the middle order intact. India went with the sheer pace of

Saini, Shami and Bumrah. It was on the Indian bowlers to keep the Aussie batsmen at bay.

The Aussie summer didn't start on an auspicious note for the Indians, the two Australian openers, David Warner and Aaron Finch had taken the Indian bowlers on remand and had stitched a partnership of 156 runs before Shami got the better of Warner.

Finch and Smith then stitched a brilliant 100-run partnership as both reached their respective hundreds and put India under immense pressure without any second thought. Smith scored 105 off 66 balls before being cleaned up by Shami. It was then on to Maxwell to take the Indian bowlers to the cleaners and show what he could do with the bat in his hand.

After a sub-par IPL, where the star all-rounder didn't hit a single six. Glenn Maxwell decided to switch on the heat and smashed a 19-ball 45 which included 3 sixes and 5 fours.

Australia posted a formidable 374 in the allotted 50 overs. The Indians had a task on their hands, it was going to be crucial to get a positive start if the Indians wanted to chase this total.

The Indians came out with all guns blazing as a wayward first over by Mitchell Starc helped India score 20 off the first over itself. But this wasn't going to continue for long as India lost 4 wickets in the first 15 overs itself, with the priced wickets of Virat Kohli and KL Rahul added onto the list.

With India in all sorts of trouble veteran opener Shikhar Dhawan and all-rounder Hardik Pandya, who was making a comeback into the Indian colors after being out due to a serious back injury, steadied the ship for India. The run rate was never a problem for the Indian team it was the wickets that weren't there.

Shikhar Dhawan played cautiously before Zampa caught hold of him and then it was Hardik who soon followed. But what was the problem, according to my understanding India could not rotate the strike at crucial junctures and also the ability to not take leverage of the good work they did until the 30th over.

India at 30 overs were 208/4 with Hardik and Shikhar going well together. But at the end of the 40th Over, India was 250/6, Adding just 42 runs and losing two crucial wickets.

Eventually, India finished the quota of 50 overs at 308/8, losing the game by 66 runs.

It was not the start the Indian team and their supporters were expecting it was a beating of the highest orders. India had to regroup and shape themselves well if they had to make a comeback in the ODI series.

2nd ODI

29th November 2020, Sydney Cricket Ground

With India being down by 1 game in the 3-match ODI series, it was on the Indian cricket team to make a comeback and make it a super Sunday and have a decider at the Manuka Oval on the 2nd of December.

Indians were trying to get over the loss they had a couple of days ago but the Australians were thinking of sealing the series with back-to-back wins at the Sydney Cricket Ground.

On a personal front, this had to be the first game where I had no idea that India was playing and trust me when I write this, I had no interest in the game. With Sanjana undergoing the surgery I was panicking no end. But life and cricket go hand in hand if something good happens in the game you feel everything is going to end well.

It was Australia who batted first again, India was going with the same 11 whereas there was one change for the Aussies. Experienced Moises Henriques came in place of Marcus Stoinis. Henriques was in the form of his life and was playing very freely in the Australian domestic circuit.

Australia was relentless in their approach, they were in no mood for relaxation, they were attacking and destroying the Indian bowling attack like they did in the first ODI, two days ago. Captain Finch and David Warner gave the team the perfect start. A start that was required by the team and which put pressure back onto the Indian bowling lineup.

Finch and Warner added 142 for the first wicket. Both completed their respective half-centuries and put pressure on the Indian bowlers. The batting was of the highest orders and the Indian team had to use Mayank Agarwal and Hardik Pandya to bow and complete the overs.

Hardik Pandya, who hadn't bowled in the IPL, was bowling for the first time after recovering from the injury, many feared that he would again get injured and might be away from the game for a few months.

On a personal note when I was browsing the score in the hospital, I felt extremely happy when I saw Hardik bowling, knowing my sister's surgery would also be fine. Hardik making his comeback with the ball, bowled well under the circumstances where everyone was being taken to the cleaners.

Steve Smith on the other hand unleashed the madman in him and went on to score a brilliant century of 62 balls which comprised 14 boundaries and 2 maximums. But this wasn't the end of the assault the batters had on the bowlers.

Glenn Maxwell was going to be the person who would perfectly complete the innings for Australia as Big Maxi scored 63 off 29 balls. This was for the second time a team's top 5 batters, scored a half-century.

The last when this incident occurred it was the same two teams playing in 2013 at Jaipur. But then, India chased down a daunting 360 with 43 balls to spare courtesy of a special knock by Virat Kohli and a brilliant century by Rohit Sharma.

This time around India had to chase 30 more than what they chased in Jaipur in the allotted 50 overs.

Indians started decently but weren't able to capitalize on the small partnerships they were making, again after giving a promising start the two openers were sent to the hut. But it was Virat Kohli and stand-in vice-captain KL Rahul who rescued the Indian team, but it wasn't going to be enough as the Indian team lost the plot and were restricted to 338/9.

Just like the previous game, it was the inability to rotate strike in the middle phase of the game that cost India the game and the series. It was all down to Canberra where the Indian team was looking to save the face and Australia was looking to do a clean sweep against the Indians.

But, if you had to ask me was I disappointed? I was sad India lost the game but I was over the moon as the operation was successful and as they say all is well that ends well.

3rd ODI

2nd December, 2022- Manuka Oval

With the series gone and a lot of talks going on the team management and Virat Kohli's captaincy and tactics. It was high time that the Indian team delivered the goods and rang in some good changes to win back the trust of the Indian fans.

India captain Virat Kohli won the toss and elected to bat first. There were a lot of changes made in both the teams. Shubman Gill, Shardul Thakur, Kuldeep Yadav, and T Natrajan were selected for the game. Gill was making a comeback into the Indian team after 1 year.

But all eyes were on the left-handed fast bowler from Tamil Nadu, T Natrajan. A bowler who wasn't given regular chances in the IPL but one good season in UAE helped Natrajan get a place in the Indian team and make his debut in the Indian colors.

On the other hand, a young Cameron Green from Western Australia was making his debut for Australia. Many pundits went on to say that Green would be the successor of Shane Watson given his exploits with the bat and the ball his ability to bat anywhere in the batting order and his ability to bowl in any given situation or condition.

A young Shubman Gill was opening the innings with the experienced Shikhar Dhawan. Gill who was in prime form in the domestic circuit was brought back into the Indian team. Gill was first seen in action at the 2018 U19 World Cup where he scored the most runs in the tournament at an average which was well over 100. Gill in the 2018 U19 World Cup not only helped the team win the trophy but also was named the Player of the tournament.

Soon after his exploits at the World Cup he was bought by Kolkata Knight Riders and continued giving good performances in the domestic season showing what he was made of and had played a few important knocks. Seeing his talent and calibre the Indian selectors decided to give the man from Punjab a debut against New Zealand in 2019, before the 50-over World Cup in England. He got a few opportunities but wasn't able to make a mark, importantly he got a taste of international cricket and understood what he had to work on and improve his quality on the highest stage.

Shikhar Dhawan was dismissed early in the innings but Gill showed what talent he had and how well he was going to grow in the coming weeks. On live television, after Shubman Gill was dismissed for a spirited and good-looking 33, Harsha Bhogle said, he has done enough to get a chance in the test series.

After the loss of Gill's wicket, India started to lose the plot and were reduced to 152/5 at the end of 32 overs. India was staring in the eyes of defeat and a clean sweep. But the duo of Hardik Pandya and Ravindra Jadeja had different plans as both the batters played a sensible knock and when required took the attack to the opposition.

Hardik Pandya and Ravindra Jadeja added 150 runs between them out of which 110 runs came in the last 10 overs as both Hardik and Jadeja took the attack to the opposition and brought back the momentum to India's side.

India ended the quota of 50 overs with 302/5 as Hardik Pandya scored a magnificent 92 off 76 balls and Ravindra Jadeja scored a well-compiled 66 off 50 balls.

There was a time when India was staring in the eyes of a clean sweep but the resilient effort from Pandya and Jadeja allowed India to come back and save themselves from the clean sweep.

And it was the case as Natarajan gave India the perfect start as he cleaned up Marnus Labuschagne and drew the first blood for the Indian team. It was just after a few overs Shardul Thakur got the all-important wicket of the in-form Steven Smith.

Australia was restricted to 56/2, it was on the shoulders of Aaron Finch to take Australia closer to the total. Australian Captain Aaron Finch and Moises Henriques tried to steady the ship but the trio of Jadeja, Kuldeep, and Shardul along with shrewd and smart captaincy brought brakes on the Australian innings and the Aussies were reduced to 158/5.

Maxwell and Alex Carey tried pulling things towards Australia but brilliant bowling changes and a level-headed understanding of the game from the bowlers assured that India wouldn't be losing the game as Australia was bundled out for 289, handing out India a victory by 13 runs.

India had saved themselves from a clean sweep but they knew if they had to go with their head held high from Australia they had to perform extremely well and play out of their skins to get the desired result.

India was now supposed to play the T20 series starting 4th December at the Manuka Oval. It was important for the Indian team to perform and change the tide of the course with a good victory. It was also a preparation for the T20 World Cup which was going to come in 2021. A good performance here would have given them an idea of who would be part of the team and what would be the team composition going into the T20 World Cup.

T20I Series

After a disappointing ODI series, India and Australia locked horns in the T20I series. India was hoping to get their team right for the T20 World Cup which was going to be held in 2021.

On the other hand, Australia was looking to attack and put more pressure on India and was trying to make them succumb under pressure so that they could be morally up in the test series, which would decide the fates of both the teams as who would be playing the finals of the World Test Championships in June.

India was in all readiness with T20 Specialists like Deepak Chahar, Sanju Samson, Washington Sundar, and Manish Pandey were part of the team. On the other hand, to tackle the Indian batting and Virat Kohli, the Aussies had summoned Mitchell Swepson into the team who would have been the second spinner and was going to be given the duty of bowling in tandem with Adam Zampa to restrict the Indian batting.

Specialists such as Andrew Tye and Daniel Sams were also a part of the team, it was also certain that either of Sams and Green would be making their T20I debut in the following series.

D'Arcy Short and Sean Abbott were also included in the star-studded Australian lineup.

1st T20I

4th December, 2020 Manuka Oval

Australian captain Aaron Finch had won the toss and elected to field first, inviting the Indians to bat first. India was all set for the game and was confident after a good recovery and comeback in the ODI series to avoid a clean sweep.

There was a T20I debut for T Natrajan as Jasprit Bumrah was suffering from a niggle and the team management didn't want him to exert much pressure as he was key to India's chances in the test series and the Indians had already lost the experienced Ishant Sharma due to an injury.

T20I specialists Manish Pandey, Deepak Chahar, Sanju Samson, and Washington Sundar were selected for the team. Indians were without Yuzvendra Chahal and Shreyas Iyer, who had been performing extremely well in the shortest format of the game.

On the other hand, Australia were extremely strong as they were loaded with superstars in their team, with the new ball being in the hands of Mitchell Starc and Josh Hazlewood and they also had 8 overs of leg spin in Adam Zampa and Mitchell Swepson.

KL Rahul was back on the top of the order as he was opening with the experienced Shikhar Dhawan. Mitch Starc had different plans and got the wicket of Shikhar Dhawan with an extremely good, unplayable yorker, which castled the southpaw.

Aaron Finch didn't waste any time and brought on the leg spinner Mitchell Swepson against his opposite number Virat Kohli, knowing how well Kohli struggles against leg spin. Australia got the all-important wicket of Kohli and India was reeling at 48/2 in 7 overs.

In came Sanju Samson, someone who had a decent good IPL, and was expected to continue his good form in the limited chances he was going to get for the Indian team to cement his place in the team.

Sanju along with Rahul tried to steady the ship for India as Indian Vice-captain completed a well-deserved half-century but it wasn't to last for long as the Indians started to lose wickets in a hurry and were restricted to 92/5 at the end of 14 overs.

It was again on the duo of Hardik Pandya and Ravindra Jadeja to save India from its blushes and honestly speaking they did their best once again. Though Hardik got out to Henriques trying to up the ante.

Jadeja didn't give up and tried to take India to rescue, he was smashing everyone who had come in his way and was playing his shots fearlessly. Jadeja was visibly injured and wasn't looking fit during his innings it was due to a hamstring pull that he had faced while running between the wickets. But a short ball from Mitchell Starc which hit Jadeja on the head gave him a concussion. It was widely discussed as many felt it was to save Jadeja's hamstring and the concussion was nothing but just a ruse.

Jadeja even after the injury scored a well-made 44 off 23 balls. With the concussion rule coming in, Ravindra Jadeja became the first Indian to be replaced by this rule and Yuzvendra Chahal became the first Indian player to be come in as a concussion substitute.

From being 114/6, Jadeja's heroics helped India reach 161 at the end of 20 overs. But was that going to be enough for the Indians?

In between the innings, there was an uproar from the Australian fans as they were extremely upset about Yuzi Chahal coming in place of the injured Ravindra Jadeja. They were crying foul as they thought that the Indians had twisted the rules in their favor and wanted a replacement for Jadeja. The Australian team management also thought that the hit on the head was very mild and wouldn't have caused a concussion and thought that the Indians were making a big deal out of it to protect Jadeja's hamstring.

D'Arcy Short and Aaron Finch opened the innings for the Aussies, and to nobody's surprise, the two Australian openers started in a good manner and tried putting pressure on the Indians. At the end of the powerplay, Australia was 53 for no loss, needing only 109 runs in the last 14 overs.

But as they say in football "Super-Sub had a different plan". Yuzi Chahal was in a mood to run through the Australian batting and was successful in doing so.

The duo of Natrajan and Chahal took 6 wickets and conceded only 55 runs in their 8 overs. India were back in the game and were back in style. The Indians bowled extremely well in the middle overs as the Australians lost the plot and at the end of 20 overs finished at 150/7, which gave India the win by 11 runs.

The concussion substitute Yuzi Chahal was adjudged Man of the Match for his valiant effort with the ball as he finished his quota of 4 overs giving away only 25 runs and taking 3 important wickets of Aaron Finch, Steven Smith, and Matthew Wade.

After a disastrous start to the ODI series, India has auspiciously started the T20I series and was well on course to do well as there was a regained energy and a regained sense of opportunity to win and perform well down under.

2nd T20I

6th December, 2022 -Sydney Cricket Ground

The stage was set for India to seal the deal and win the T20 series. It was also necessary for India to make some amends to the team to avoid the same batting collapse that happened in the first T20I at Canberra.

Australia had ringed in some changes, Aaron Finch was replaced by Matthew Wade as the captain of the team, Daniel Sams was making his debut, and T20I specialist Andrew Tye was making the team for the game at SCG.

India on the other hand had gone in with two changes Manish Pandey was replaced by Shreyas Iyer and Shami was replaced by Shardul Thakur.

Australia was batting first and just like the first game had started well, the stand-in captain Wade upped the ante and took the attack to the opposition as he targeted both Chahar and Sundar. Eventually D'Arcy Short was out courtesy of some brilliant bowling by Natarajan.

India was feeling the pressure as Australia had piled up 59 in the first 6 overs. India was desperately looking for a wicket as both Smith and Wade were batting brilliantly and were rotating the strike and taking the attack to the bowlers by hitting a boundary whenever the opportunity was presented.

Matthew Wade was in some cracking form as he scored a magnificent 50 off just 25 balls. The innings by Matthew Wade was a showcase of class and power which helped Australia get a brilliant start. But the dismissal of Wade was a comical one.

It was the last ball of the 8th over when Virat Kohli had dropped a lollipop catch of Matthew Wade of Washington Sundar's bowling, but Virat was quick to rectify his mistake as the Indian captain saw the opportunity of running out his opposite number and threw the ball to the strikers end where Wade was caught napping, thus bringing an end to a fantastic 32 balls 58 by Matthew Wade.

Australia was in great command of the game and was dictating the pace of the game, they were set for a big total which would have been well above 200, but some great bowling by Natarajan helped India restrict the Aussies to a total of 194 in the allotted 20 overs.

Apart from Natarajan, every other Indian bowler had been taken to the cleaners by the Australian batters.

The onus was now on the Indian batters and especially the openers to give India a fantastic start so that the mammoth total of 194 could be chased down.

It was also the same ground where India chased down a mammoth total of 190 in 2016, where Virat Kohli, Suresh Raina, and Yuvraj Singh were the heroes of the chase.

KL Rahul and Shikhar Dhawan came to open the innings and to nobody's surprise had started extremely well, which put the Australian bowlers under tremendous pressure and there was a need to take wickets.

Andrew Tye who is considered to be a T20 specialist drew the first blood as India lost their first wicket at the score of 56. India ended the powerplay on a high, with 60 on the board.

With India's intent against spin being conservative, Mitchell Swepson and Adam Zampa bowled their overs quickly without being taken for plenty of runs. In this while Shikhar Dhawan compiled a well-made half-century before getting out to Adam Zampa.

Swepson then got the wicket of Sanju Samson and India was reeling at 120/3, needing another 75 more to win in the last 6 overs. In came Hardik Pandya, who was given the responsibility to finish the game along with Virat Kohli.

Pandya had been in fine touch in the white ball leg and was hoping to finish the game and seal the series for India.

During this Virat Kohli played a shot of Andrew Tye, which went for a six but reminded the world of his very good friend AB De Villiers. Virat had scooped the ball over the fine-leg fielder into the sea of blue.

Kohli and Pandya looked set and were looking in full flow to take India home, but the debutant Daniel Sams got the all-important wicket of Virat Kohli, 45 remaining for India to win the game.

It was now on the shoulders of Hardik and Shreyas to take India home, and both batted sensibly took their chances, and made sure that India wasn't pushed way back in the game.

Debutant Daniel Sams was given the responsibility to bowl the last over and had the onus of defending 14 off the final 6 balls. Hardik on the other hand had the experience of chasing down these kinds of totals in the final overs, taking the leaf out of his idol's book. Hardik decided to take the matter into his own hands and decided to finish the game with 2 sixes off 3 balls to seal the deal for the Indians.

With Pandya's flourish, with support from Virat Kohli and Shikhar Dhawan, the Indian team won yet another T20I series down under. This victory was not only a statement but also a message to the Australians that the Indians are slow starters, but once they find their groove, they are difficult to contain.

Hardik Pandya for his great performance and exploits with the bat which helped India finish the game was awarded the Man of the Match.

With the win in the second T20I, the Indians had their eyes set on the clean sweep. It was going to be interesting to see if the Indians would complete their second T20I clean sweep on Australian soil in 4 years.

3rd T20I

8th December, 2022 – Sydney Cricket Ground

With the series already clinched by the Indians, the team was ready to repeat the clean sweep of 2016. There were a few positives for Indians in the series and the best of all the positives was the emergence of T Natarajan.

India as a team was always looking for a left-handed pacer, and with his exploits in the death, India had an advantage. If only Natarajan had been able to remain fit for a long period, Bumrah and Natarajan would have made a deadly combination that would have restricted the opposition from scoring freely at the end of the innings.

Aaron Finch was making a comeback into the Aussie team for the final T20I, whereas the Indians were going with the same team and had no plans of changing the winning combination.

With Australia batting first the hosts needed to continue their form at the top of the innings, but things went down the hill as Washington Sundar in his first over got the wicket of the Australian captain Aaron Finch.

But Matthew Wade was in no mood to give away his good form and the wicket-keeper batsman kept the Indian bowlers at bay with his attacking batting and attacking approach. With Smith taking a more conservative approach to his batting he tried to keep things simple by supporting Wade and played a run-a-ball inning before getting bamboozled by Washington Sundar.

India had good control of the game but a 90-run partnership between Wade and Maxwell, helped Australia reach a competitive total of 186. Wade played a fantastic innings of 80 which included 7 fours and 2 maximums. On the other hand, Maxwell continued his love affair against India at Sydney Cricket Ground as he scored a fantastic, 54 off just 36 balls which included 3 fours and 3 sixes.

Washington Sundar was the pick of the bowlers as he finished his quota of 4 overs picking 2 wickets and conceding only 34.

India had to chase 187, to get the clean sweep but the Aussies were in no mood to give away the game as they had their plans set and knew that the Indians could be put under pressure if the spin duo of Zampa and Swepson could take some quick wickets without giving any runs.

Captain Aaron Finch decided to throw the first over to Glenn Maxwell, and it turned out to be a great decision as the Australians got the prized wicket of KL Rahul in the first over itself.

India needed to pull their socks up and the captain and experienced Dhawan oversaw controlling and steadying the ship. Kohli and Dhawan took the total to 55 in the powerplay. India was on course of chasing the total but the spin duo of Zampa and Swepson were in action again.

India's approach towards spin was causing them problems as both the spinners, choked the flow of runs and caused problems for the Indians and the chances of India getting the win also seemed a little bleak.

But, the legend of Virat Kohli was still there, batting and smashing hoping that he could take the team home and get India the clean sweep and become the first team to clean sweep Australia twice in a T20I series.

Virat Kohli looked well set but wasn't getting any support from his other teammates as players were coming and going on the other trying to up the scoring rate and getting close to the target, set by the Aussies.

Swepson and Zampa bowled 7 overs and conceded only 44 runs taking 4 wickets between them. They took the important wickets of Shikhar Dhawan, Sanju Samson, Shreyas Iyer, and the hero of the last game Hardik Pandya.

Virat Kohli played one of the most eventful knocks in a lost cause as the Indian captain scored 85 off 61 balls before getting dismissed by Andrew Tye in the 19th over. Kohli's knock gave him the confidence to score runs and even the century that eluded him in the year 2020.

India eventually lost the game falling short of the target by 12 runs. India had already won the series but a victory in the final game would have given them even more satisfaction and happiness.

Mitchell Swepson was adjudged the man of the match for his match-winning spell where he took three wickets and only conceded 23 runs in his quota of 4 overs.

Hardik Pandya was adjudged man of the series for his fantastic performance with the bat in the series, but the star Indian all-rounder did something very heartfelt that won the hearts of everyone around the world and received immense love and respect for his gesture. Hardik gave his Man of the Series trophy to the debutant T Natrajan who had performed extremely well in his debut T20 series.

It was a great series for the Indians and their preparation for the T20 World Cup was on track. But with the T20I series done and dusted, it was on to the greatest event of the series. It was time to gear for the Border-Gavaskar Trophy.

In 2018, the Indians won their first-ever test series on Australian soil. But, it was not going to be easy for the Indians to repeat the victory of 2018. Indians had to step up and perform extremely well to win the series and create history.

Was it going to be easy, we never know. But whatever was going to happen, the whole world would go on to remember that no matter what.

BORDER – GAVASKAR TROPHY

The stage was set, Test cricket was on the brink of its return, and the world with eyes glued to their television sets was in all readiness to witness a cracker jacker of a series between two great test teams. Teams that took pride in playing the hardest and the longest format of the game. Two teams that emphasized test cricket, were going head-to-head against each other.

For India, it was to show the world that they could defeat Australians again on their home turf and prove to the world that it was not just luck that helped them win the Border Gavaskar trophy in 2018.

For the mighty Australians, it was to take the revenge of the bitter loss in 2018-19. The Australians were boosted this time around with the inclusion of Steve Smith and David Warner, which meant that the Australians had a strong batting lineup that was going to be supported by a great bowling unit in Pat Cummins, Mitchell Starc, Josh Hazlewood, and Nathan Lyon.

India on the other hand was depleted as the Indians didn't have the services of their star opener Rohit Sharma, who would only return to the team after the second test, and didn't have the services of Ishant Sharma, who was the star of the series in 2018-19.

Ishant Sharma was a big loss for the Indians, as the veteran Indian pacer had played 4 tours in Australia and was on the verge of playing his 100th test if he was fully fit for the Australian series. In India's series victory in 2018, Ishant played a major part. The pacer from

Delhi had taken 11 wickets in 3 test matches at a commendable average of 23.82.

The other major concern for India was the departure of Virat Kohli after the pink ball test in Adelaide. The Indian skipper had requested the BCCI to release him from the squad after the first test as a part of paternity leave. Virat Kohli had made it very clear that he wanted to be with his family during the delivery of his baby.

There were talks about India repeating their heroics of 2018-19, and pundits from all over the world were certain if India didn't win in Adelaide, it could be a whitewash for the Indians, and Australia could take the revenge for 2018, happily and easily.

It was up to the Indians to start on an auspicious note, to give themselves a cushion if anything goes wrong in the absence of Virat Kohli and Ishant Sharma.

The Indians had selected a very balanced squad and had selected pacers of different varieties and kinds for the test series.

Indian Squad for the test series:

Virat Kohli, Ajinkya Rahane, KL Rahul, Mayank Agarwal, Prithvi Shaw, Cheteshwar Pujara, Hanuma Vihar, Rishabh Pant, Wridhimann Saha, Ravindra Jadeja, Ravichandran Ashwin, Jasprit Bumrah, Mohammed Shami, Mohammed Siraj, Umesh Yadav, Kuldeep Yadav, Navdeep Saini, Rohit Sharma, Shubman Gill

Reserves: Ishan Porel, Kartik Tyagi, T Natarajan, Shardul Thakur, Washington Sundar and Shreyas Iyer.

Mohammed Siraj and Navdeep Saini were called up for the first time for a test series, there were a lot of talks about how the two pacers would bowl in the Australian conditions, but with the pace and seam bowling the two possessed if given a chance both would do extremely well.

It was a fairy tale story for Shubman Gill and Mohammed Siraj. Two players coming from two parts of the country but had the utmost passion and love for the game of cricket, it was on them to perform well, whenever the chance beckoned on the two.

Gill, a top-order batsman was the talk of the town, a stylish young man from Punjab. Shubman carried his charm and charisma. With pundits speaking good about the young man a lot depended on how he would make use of the chances given to him when Virat Kohli wouldn't be there.

On the other hand, Siraj had already made his debut for India in two formats and had played a few games but hadn't shown what he was made up of. With Siraj's selection causing confusion and anguish, it was to be understood that the two formats were completely different and the red ball cricket and white ball cricket were two different ball games in all and any literal sense. With Siraj being with the Indian team, he got the news of his father passing away. In COVID times with the bio bubble and restrictions being at their peak it was going to be difficult for the Hyderabad-born fast bowler to visit his father's funeral and comeback. With a lot at stake, it was a surety that Siraj would make his test debut if any of the premier fast bowlers got injured during the course of the test series.

On paper, the Australians were looking more stable and strong as compared to the Indians which was understandable as the injuries and departures of a few key players made India look weak on paper, but it is a well-known fact about India that whenever their backs are to the wall they give it their all to turn the table and win games from hopeless or to say less hopeful situations.

Before the pink ball test in Adelaide, India played two warm-up games in Sydney to get a feel of how the pitch would play during the series. It was going to be extremely important for India to play the two warm-up games properly as there was a place in the finals of the World Test Championship at stake and the Indians could not afford any slip-ups whatsoever if the Indian team wanted to smooth passage to the World Test championship finals.

India A vs Australia A

1st Practice game

The Indians played the warm game under the leadership of Ajinkya Rahane as Virat Kohli and company were busy with the limited-overs leg and these players needed to get a feel of the conditions. The reiteration on the conditions is only because of the bio bubble and the pitch conditions, ground dimensions, and weather are quite different as compared to what it is in India. Also, the type of ball that is used in Australia is the Kookaburra, whereas in India the SG ball is used.

India was batting first in the practice game and to everyone's horror didn't start on an auspicious note as both the openers Shubman Gill and Prithvi Shaw were out for duck and the Indian score read 6/2.

It was then on the senior pros to take the game ahead and help India reach a respectable total and the bowlers could have something to bowl and that is what happened as the senior pros Cheteshwar Pujara and Ajinkya Rahane. Pujara played a handy knock of 54 which was nicely doubled by Rahane with an unbeaten 117.

A thing that had to be understood was that it was very important for Cheteshwar Pujara to find his groove because when India toured Australia in 2018, it was Pujara who batted and batted all day long just to irritate the Aussie bowlers.

Hazlewood had once famously said we don't talk about Pujara in the team meeting because we have seen the man all day long and can't afford to spoil our moods because we know the man is not going to get out to whatever is bowled at him.

If India had to do well in the series, India was going to be heavily dependent on this warrior of a player named Cheteshwar Pujara.

India declared the innings at 247. The Aussies in return scored 306 courtesy of a magnificent century from the wonder boy Cameron Green. Umesh and Siraj were the pick of the bowlers for India as both the Indian pacers took 3 wickets apiece.

Siraj bowled extremely well in the given opportunities which meant that he knew his way around the red ball and was not going to be an easy bowler to bat to.

India in the second innings crumbled as the Indians could only score 189, with no time in the game left the Australians couldn't go for the win and the game ended in a draw.

There were a lot of takeaways for India from the first game and a few positives included Siraj's bowling and Pujara's and Rahane's batting. But there was a big concern for the Indian team that was the opening pair, Mayank was a surety but would Shaw find touch and score good runs or would it be wise to throw Shubman Gill in the deep waters and have him tested against Starc, Hazlewood, and Cummins.

There were a few question marks but the best thing was India had another warm-up game to get all the answers and set a team that could repeat the feat of 2018-19.

2nd Practice Game- Pink Ball Test

The First test of the Border Gavaskar trophy was going to be played at Adelaide which was going to be a pink ball test, and the Indians needed to practice with the pink ball to understand the conditions and especially how to bat during the dusk period of the day and also under the lights with the swinging pink ball.

It was the last opportunity for Prithvi Shaw to prove his mantle and to get a nod ahead of Shubman Gill in the team that would play the first game at Adelaide. Prithvi Shaw is one of those players who I see as a player with a lot of potential and have immense respect for. Speaking on personal terms, I feel Shaw is one of those players when given a chance to play for India and if given a longer run would perform in the manner he is expected to.

If we see Shaw and the way he bats he has the class of a complete batsman but also has that aggressive game of someone like Virender Sehwag or David Warner who could cause problems for the opposition in the first session or the initial overs of a test match.

In this particular Practice game, India was again batting first and Shaw was opening with the in-form Mayank Agarwal, to everyone's expectation Shaw batted the way he was expected to smashing and hitting through the covers and playing the same straight drives which reminded anyone and everyone of the legendary Sachin Tendulkar. The simple idea that Shaw had in his batting was to take the lacquer off that beautiful pink ball. Shaw somewhat was successful in providing that before being cleaned up by Will Sutherland for 40.

His 40 came in just 29 balls which consisted of 8 crisp-looking boundaries. His deputy from the 2018 U19 World Cup which India won scored a good-looking 43, before the Indian middle order crumbled and was reduced to 123 for 9.

With India 123/9, everyone was expecting India to be bundled out very soon but a certain Indian cricketer known for his fierce bowling and not very well known for his batting named Jasprit Bumrah took the bowlers to the cleaners.

Bumrah was batting like any other senior batter, it felt like Virat Kohli or Rishabh Pant had transferred his power to him, he was crunching, smashing hitting, pulling sweeping the bowlers like he had been a batter all his life and it was just the bowling which was shown to the world.

Bumrah piled up his first-ever First-class 50 and en route scored an unbeaten 55, he smashed 6 beautiful boundaries and 2 maximums. India were bundled out for 194. Thanks to Bumrah's and Siraj's partnership India put up a modest but a decent looking total on the board.

It was up to the bowlers to show their class with the pink ball and with the ball being extremely new, use the lacquer of the Kookaburra to perfect use. And, that is what happened Bumrah along with Shami and Navdeep Saini did the same, didn't give the Australian batters any reprieve, and bundled the Australia A squad for just a mere 108, courtesy 3 wickets apiece for both Saini and Shami and 2 wickets for India's Talisman Jasprit Bumrah.

It was now onto the batters to put up a good show in the second innings and with the pitch getting better to bat on it was going to be a case of just having the heads on the shoulder and not doing anything extravagant which could cause trouble to the Indian team.

Agarwal and Gill scored a brilliant half-century proving that it was about application and the pitch was getting extremely good to bat on. Hanuma Vihari who was playing at 4 played with utmost understanding and application understanding what it is like to play under pressure and scored a brilliant hundred proving that he was going to be a mainstay in the Indian team for this test series.

Just before the start of the series, India captain Virat Kohli in an interview with Steve Smith had said Hanuma Vihari would be a player to look out for in the series because of what he provided to the team.

Hanuma Vihari made his debut for India in 2018 when India was touring England, and ever since then, he has been a mainstay in India's batting lineup given what he provided to the team with the bat and the great skill he had of batting with the tail and bailing India out of difficult periods just like his predecessor VVS Laxman used to do. The added benefit of Hanuma Vihari was that the man could bowl a few overs of spin and if required could be used as a partnership breaker. Not to forget Hanuma Vihari's first-ever test wicket was of the great Sir Alistair Cook who was looking in great touch and had scored a magnificent ton in that game.

Alongside Vihari, there was another man named Rishabh Pant, the fearless evergreen Rishabh Pant, someone who has no fear of the bowler the swinging ball, or per se the conditions in general. Rishabh Pant made his plans clear he was not going to respect the bowling lineup he was going to go full throttle and be fearless against the bowlers. Pant scored a magnificent ton which was brought up in only 73 balls which included 9 boundaries and 6 magnificent sixes.

Rishabh Pant who had a below-par IPL in UAE was dropped from the white ball setup, but knowing what the man could do in test cricket and how well he could change the game it was necessary to have Rishabh Pant in the test squad. It shouldn't be forgotten that he played a graceful, counter-attacking knock of 150 against the same team in Sydney.

It was to be understood that if Rishabh Pant could play 60-70 balls without losing his concentration, he could bat the opposition out of the game and that is what Rishabh Pant had in him and there was a very peculiar record which Rishabh had under his belt that he had scored 6 consecutive 25+ scores against Australia in test cricket which was previously done only by one batsman and that was the legendary Sir Vivian Richards.

Rishabh's inclusion in the team could have meant that he would go behind the spinner and Australia having just one spin bowling option would mean that it would be mayhem for the Aussies.

India declared the second innings at 386/4 courtesy centuries from Vihari and counter-attacking knock from Rishabh Pant and half-centuries from Mayank Agarwal and Shubman Gill.

The game ended in a draw as Ben McDermott and Jack Wildermuth batted all day long to push a draw.

India had done extremely well in all three departments in this particular game, it was now time that India performed well in the test series against Australia which started in Adelaide on the 17th of December.

It was time for a big showdown, the 4 match test series was going to be a fight for supremacy, bring back the lost laurel, and a fight to show that which team is the best in the world. But more than that what I felt was that this test series was going to play an important role in making people happy, satisfied, and secure at the same time. With the COVID-19 virus at its peak in India, it was time that people could deviate their minds from the Virus and focus on what could be a good test series.

FIRST TEST- BORDER GAVASKAR TROPHY

ADELAIDE OVAL, 17th December - 21st December, 2021

The stage was set, it was time for the big one it was time that two heavyweights after all the practice and hard work met each other in the test series.

This was not only a test series but it could be a ticket for a final for both the teams, as both the teams were in the fray of a place in the finals of the World Test Championship, which was scheduled to be played in June 2021.

India was confident of repeating their feat of 2018 and Australia was ready to take revenge for what had happened back then. Australians were confident of doing well as their two talisman Steve Smith and David Warner were back in the team after completing their suspension.

India on the other hand was without two of their experienced players Rohit Sharma and Ishant Sharma. For me what I felt before the series was that of the two Sharma's missing India would miss Ishant more given his experience, record, and understanding of the Australian conditions. If Ishant had toured Australia in 2020/21, it would have been his 5h Tour Down Under.

On the other hand, the Australian media, who have a habit of glorifying things way too much, glorified it was going to be Virat vs Australia and it was Virat's homecoming to his favorite cricket ground. Virat Kohli always had a good relationship with Adelaide,

He scored his first-ever test ton at Adelaide, and captained India for the first time in Adelaide in 2014 where the man scored centuries in both innings, and not to forget that test win in 2018, he had it all. There was a sense of homecoming for the Indian Captain, but was it going to be easy that was the question. Pink ball, Kohli departed after the test series to be with his wife as the couple were expectant parents.

It was 16th December 2022 – India had announced their playing XI, to everyone's surprise, the Indian team had dropped both Rishabh Pant and Ravindra Jadeja from the playing XI. What was surprising was that Jadeja who had a fantastic white ball series had been dropped from the team, many were anticipating it was the injury he had sustained in the 1st T20I at Manuka Oval, Canberra. Rishabh's omission was not a surprise as the Indians needed a keeper who could keep well in the difficult Aussie Conditions to pacers of Bumrah, Shami, and Umesh Yadav's quality.

India's Playing XI:

Mayank Agarwal, Prithvi Shaw, Cheteshwar Pujara, Virat Kohli, Ajinkya Rahane, Hanuma Vihari, Wridhhiman Saha, Ravichandran Ashwin, Mohammed Shami, Jasprit Bumrah, Umesh Yadav.

Australia's Playing XI:

Joe Burns, Matthew Wade, Marnus Labuschagne, Steve Smith, Travis Head, Cameron Green, Tim Paine, Pat Cummins, Mitchell Starc, Nathan Lyon, and Josh Hazlewood.

On the day of the game as anticipated there was a lot of commotion, commotion on how India would play in these conditions as India had only played one test and had won that game in dominating fashion against Bangladesh at the historic Eden Gardens, where the Indian

Captain Virat Kohli had scored a century and hadn't scored a century ever since people were anticipating King Kohli as they like to call him to end his century drought and also get the series going with his fierce and never die attitude. On the other hand, the Aussies had played 7 pink ball tests before this historic test and had not lost a single game. It was going to be a fierce test match and everyone was sensing the same.

The toss happened and to nobody's surprise after winning the toss India elected and decided to bat first. It was the first test match for Prithvi Shaw in Australia. Prithvi known for his prowess was a batsman everyone was looking forward to seeing and witnessing how he could play in these conditions. India's coach and everyone's favorite Ravi Shastri on the eve of the test match commented that the Mumbai lad is a mixture of Sehwag's power, Sachin's class, and Lara's technique. But the question was could the young man prove his critics wrong and his coach and his fans including me who rate him so highly correct and give them bragging rights against the critics?

DAY 1

The stage was set, players were ready India's Jana Gana Mana was played with great pride and then Australia's Advance Australia Fair was played. To all the player's pride and emotion the game was set to begin and in high anticipation, it was the two Indian openers who took center stage for India. Prithvi Shaw and Mayank Agarwal took the stage and were ready to roar. Left-arm Fast bowler Mitchell Starc had the ball in hand and was ready to rock the world for the Indians.

The second ball of the test, and something that all Indian fans were afraid of happened Inside edge and bowled, Shaw's technique of keeping the bat away from the body and pads was exposed, and this time it was exposed heavily and he had to pay a price of losing his wicket. The Aussies were excited and had drawn the first blood.

In came a man who every Australian was afraid of and didn't want to talk about. The ever-dependent Indian wall had come onto the ground and he was ready to take the game away from the Australians by just standing and taking out the lacquer from the ball, he was motivated and was in the mood to take away the game, but at this particular moment the challenge was different it was not going to be the same as it was in 2018, where he batted and batted and made the ball old. Here he was facing bowlers under conditions which would be utilized and the ball which would swing a little more than what is expected.

Mayank Agarwal and Cheteshwar Pujara made a pact and decided that they wouldn't touch the ball which is moving and doing too much, they would wait for the odd bad ball and hit them accordingly, for them it was more about irritating the Australian bowlers than actually working the scorecard because they knew once the bowlers start getting tired and they would get loose balls and they would be able to capitalize and get the runs.

Pujara had become a wall he wasn't trying to do much but was just trying to get the first hour of play done without losing any other wicket and give India breathing space so that the batsmen who were next in line could get into the zone and get the runs at a faster and a quicker rate.

Mayank was hitting the odd boundaries and running hard before he got an unplayable delivery from Pat Cummins which castled him as the ball hit the top of the middle stump and he was gone, for 17, you would sense that India would have been in trouble but according to me and my understanding I feel that this was the best position for India to be in and with experienced batters like Kohli and Rahane still to come, India could have reached the 300 run mark as the Indians would have taken all day long to just tire the Australians.

After the dismissal of Mayank Agarwal came the King, the king who rules Adelaide as if it were Karol Bagh of Delhi, Churchgate of Mumbai, or Cubbon Park of Bangalore. Virat Kohli had come knowing that this going to be his last outing in Australia for this series. For Virat, it was very important to understand that the scenario was critical and he had to make a partnership with Cheteshwar Pujara, the first idea was to play till lunch and then take the score to a hundred. For them, at that particular moment, it was very important to set small targets and accomplish them so that they could shift the pressure back to the Aussies.

India at lunch hadn't lost any other wicket and were 41/2. A serious session was going to come as the second session could set the tone for the test match and maybe even the series. The Indian team had a lot to play for and knew a small mistake would cause a lot of issues and difficulties.

Virat and Pujara had understood the task and were putting the pressure back on the bowlers knowing that spin would be introduced from one end and the fourth pacer in debutant Cameron Green whom the press was referring to as "Wonderboy from Perth" would be bowling the pressure and the momentum could be shifted, understanding the task the Indians started to accumulate the runs, slowly and steadily at the 30 over mark India reached to the first milestone 50.

Virat then started to take the pressure on the Aussies by taking boundaries and also started to rotate the strike, with Virat on the crease and the long Australian boundaries singles being converted to double is just a mere formality and Kohli will make his partner run as much as he can.

The two were looking good as they put on a partnership of 50 runs and took the score to 100, India was looking to score steadily and India was on course to do the same. But as often we see in cricket against the run of play India lost a wicket and they lost a big wicket of Cheteshwar Pujara who was caught at leg gully by Marnus Labuschagne.

India was now 100/3 when the vice-captain Ajinkya Rahane joined the Indian captain, the two had a big task on their hands as they had to take the game along and start scoring freely only to give the batters after them a cushion to play freely without any pressure.

Ajinkya and Virat have always had a great understanding with each other and who could forget when the two took the Aussie bowlers to the cleaners in 2014 and how well both negated the Australian bowlers in that 2014/15 Border Gavaskar Trophy. This was a perfect stage for both of them to score big and give it to the Aussies who were bowling hostile lengths and were not giving anything freely to the Indian batters.

Virat was playing freely and had reached his half-century in 123 balls which had some brilliant shots and consisted of 5 boundaries en route to his brilliant 50. He was looking good along with his favorite partner as both of them were looking to tuck the ones and two and get the odd boundaries, India's run rate in the third session had increased and India was looking to capitalise on the partnership between the two experienced campaigners.

But in came a moment that not only changed the course of the innings but also changed the course of the test match and if I want to add on changed the course of the whole series.

It was the last ball of the 76th Over, Lyon was bowling to Ajinkya Rahane and he played a checked drive to the fielder at mid-off, Rahane took a few steps towards the non-striker and Kohli obliged, and only a few moments later he was halfway down the pitch had no way to get back into the crease. Kohli was run out in the most Un-

Kohli-like way. He was extremely dejected and couldn't believe what had happened, India was looking extremely good and was looking to end the day on a high with Kohli and Rahane carrying the bat till the end of the play, but it wasn't meant to be. Kohli was dismissed for a well-made 74 as India lost their way after the fall of Kohli's wicket and it was Rahane who followed Kohli and India ended the day with 233 for the loss of 6 wickets.

If you take the review of the first day it was a day that had some nerve-wracking moments and also had some good cricket on display, the game, was evenly balanced with Wriddhiman Saha and Ravichandran Ashwin would have been the batters who would be coming on Day 2 to continue the batting for the Indian team.

DAY 2

India started the day with an overnight score of 233/6 it was a chance for the Indians to reach 260 and put the pressure on the Australians as the pitch was assisting the bowlers and it needed a long stint of Pujara-esque patience to score runs on this pitch.

But to the Indian fan's horror and the way Indian Tail had performed in the last 3 years the same thing happened, the tail did not hang around for a long time and Hazlewood and Company finished the tail as the Indians could only add 11 more to their overnight total and were bundled out for 244.

The score was below par but given the Indian pacers, we knew that the Indian pacers could extract great assistance from the pitch, and given Jasprit Bumrah's and Shami's form India was confident of giving back it to the Australians. It was going to be a battle of patience and who was going to drop the patience test first?

Australians on the other hand knew that they couldn't underestimate the Indian pace attack and the wily old fox in Ashwin as they knew the conditions and were confident to make it a difficult task for the Australians to take a lead.

In walked Matthew Wade and Joe Burns for Australia and the ball was in the hands of two experienced Indian bowlers Umesh Yadav and Jasprit Bumrah, they key for the Indians was going to be early wickets as they could make early inroads which could expose Australian middle order, which would prompt the Indian captain Virat Kohli to bring in Ravi Ashwin who had a fantastic record against Steve Smith.

Wade and Burns were both extremely cautious in the start not doing anything extravagant and not doing anything unnecessary, they were keeping it extremely simple taking singles and not giving anything to the Indian pacers.

India's trump card Bumrah did what he had been doing for the last 4 months. He was bowling on beautiful length which was testing both the openers and was causing difficulty for both Wade and Burns, India needed a breakthrough, and no one better than Bumrah provided the breakthrough. Bumrah bowled a beautiful inswinger to which Matthew Wade had no answers and was plumb in front of the stumps. India had got the start they wanted, they had drawn the first blood but Bumrah's engine was just heating up as in the next over India's talisman got the second wicket of Joe Burns, and suddenly Australia was reeling at 29 for 2.

But to Australia's delight their two premier batters were there on the crease Marnus Labuschagne and Steven Smith, and seeing the opportunity the Indian Captain brought on his spinner in Ashwin. Ravi Ashwin had Steve Smith in his pocket during the IPL as the former Aussie captain wasn't able to score freely against Ashwin and he was out to Ashwin on both occasions when the two faced each other. Ashwin was bowling steadily and trying to make Smith play the wrong lines and was trying to get him out in the slips. The field was packed for Smith as there was a slip stationed short leg, a leg slip, and also a fielder at mid-wicket to get Smith out. India was aggressive in their thought process here, and as Kohli has always been he was aggressive in his field placements and the bowling changes, India was bossing the game at the moment, so it was very important for India to take a couple of wickets and put the Aussies on the back foot.

As the game progressed Ashwin was getting some assistance from the pitch, he was turning the ball and a pure off-spinner ball that skidded through quickly got the outside edge of Smith's bat and went straight into the hands of Ajinkya Rahane at first slip. India was delighted by the performance; India was ruling the game now. India now had a chance to take over the game and put pressure and Australia and rightly so the Indians didn't leave even one page unturned and restricted the Australians to 79/5 as Ashwin wreaked havoc.

Labuschagne and captain Tim Paine had a task on their hands, to build a partnership and rightly so they built a partnership and kept small targets to reduce the deficit and exposed India's problem of cleaning up the tail quickly, which the Indians were not capable of doing.

The partnership was going on well and for India to take a wicket it had become a necessity, at that time India's most trusted Umesh Yadav who was known to be a force with the old ball was brought into the attack to get some reverse swing and as anticipated Umesh was able to get some reverse swing and he was able to break the partnership as he caught Marnus Labuschagne plumb in front of the stumps. Marnus played a fantastic knock of 47 under difficult and testing conditions where the pink ball was doing a little bit too much.

The onus was on Tim Paine, as he had to build partnerships with every batter and had to make sure that the Aussies didn't falter and brought the deficit as close as possible.

Paine was playing a counter-attacking knock and he was seen to be in an aggressive mode he was smashing the boundaries of each of the three fast bowlers and was not giving it away easily. He received extensive support from first Starc who held one end and batted with him for as many as 7 overs and Lyon who was with him for another 6 overs but the pressure back on India.

Courtesy Umesh Yadav India was able to bowl out Australia and the Aussies were bundled out for 191 handing India a lead of 53 runs, India would have wanted to bowl them out a little early but they would have taken this with both hands as this could give them the confidence they required going into the second innings.

Ashwin was the pick of the bowlers for India as the off-spinner took 4 wickets and Tim Paine was the highest scorer for Australia as the Aussie captain scored a brilliant unbeaten 73 off 99 balls which consisted of 10 boundaries.

Now the challenge was going to come for India, they had to survive the twilight and 6 overs remaining in Day 2. Prithvi Shaw and Mayank Agarwal had a task on their hands and they had to perform extremely well for the next 6 overs as India would have loved to go unbeaten.

Starc opened the bowling for Australia, the Indians had a tentative start the only thing going their heads was to survive the day, and then when they came to bat on Day 3 they could solidify and build on the lead they had.

But to disappoint everyone, Prithvi Shaw was rattled by a brilliant inswinging ball by Pat Cummins and India had lost their first wicket with 17 balls remaining in the day's play. Now you must be thinking Cheteshwar Pujara might have come to bat or maybe Virat Kohli would have come to bat. To everyone's surprise and to make the meme world go ecstatic, Jasprit Bumrah came to bat at 3. He had a big task on hand as he had to survive the next three overs of steaming Starc and Cummins, he was able to do it and was extremely successful in doing that.

India ended the day at 9/1 with a lead of 62 going to the third day. The third day was going to be extremely important as it was going to be the moving day and was going to decide the fate of the test match and who would win round 1 of the 4-match test series between the rivals.

Were we in for a sweet surprise or a shock that would change how Indian cricket would think and play? You'll soon find out.

DAY 3

It was a bright sunny day in Adelaide on 19th December 2020. India was looking to capitalize on the lead they had got and knew that if they could set a total of somewhere between 250-300 it would have been game on and India would be able to dictate terms and could be able to take the lead. The Indian fans and media were sure that India would be able to take a good fruitful lead and would be able to corner the mighty Australians.

I vividly remember, there were a few meme pages that went overboard and said " Ohh god when we wake up in the morning make sure that, Mayank Agarwal is at 100 and Jasprit Bumrah is batting on 99, and I can see the greatest 100's of all times"

But Cummins and Hazlewood had different plans and while writing this part it still gives me goosebumps on how the heck this even happened. In came Cummins bowling took Jasprit Bumrah in the first over of the spell, India was reduced to 15/2, and early in the piece came India's Mr.Dependable the master of tough situations, but the situation was extremely difficult and tough the ball was swinging and the batters had no idea on how to play the bowling attack.

The Pink ball was doing too much for the liking of the batters and the Indian batters were continuously playing out maiden overs to reduce the pressure, but as soon as they thought they had gotten over the difficult phase in came Josh Hazlewood, who partnered with Pat Cummins to destroy India and reduce India to 15/5 and then simultaneously to 19/6.

It was extremely difficult for us to understand what was going on, on a cold winter morning we were extremely confused as to what happened and what was going on. The things were really hard to comprehend because a team of India's caliber which has the batting prowess and consists of a middle order that has Pujara, Kohli, and Rahane had found themselves reeling on 19/6, Hazlewood and Cummins ran through the Indian batting lineup. India was looking at the lowest total ever made in a test match by them, India had scored 42 against England at Lord's in 1942 and it seemed as if the record would be broken after Hanuma Vihari was gone for 8 and the score was reading 31/9.

Umesh Yadav and Mohammed Shami had an uphill task to save themselves from the blushes but something very extraordinary happened and the Indian fast bowler Mohammed Shami was hit on the forearm by Pat Cummins, and it seemed like he had broken his bowling arm. Shami had to retire hurt and the Indian Innings ended at 36, which was India's lowest total in Test Cricket.

Pat Cummins and Josh Hazlewood had run riot against the Indians and the Indians had no clue about it. Indians were bundled out for 36 in just 21.2 overs.

The Indian scorecard read 4,9,2,0,4,0,8,4,0,4,1 it seemed like a telephone number and the Indian team had no clue as to what had happened. The fans were confused, the media was trying to understand what had happened and if you had seen the player's face they were extremely dejected and had no idea what had happened, clueless, sad, and dejected.

If you put the scenario in Hindi, it was a case of " Aaya Ram, Gaya Ram"

The Australians were set a target of 90 to take a lead in the Border-Gavaskar Trophy and nothing surprising the Australians batted sensibly didn't take too many risks played on the bruise of the Indian players and were successful in chasing the meek target of 90.

Australia was 1-0 up what was next for India, Virat Kohli was going on paternity leave and Mohammed Shami was injured now, two potential debuts were lined up for India, but was it enough to get India back on track?

For now, India had no clue as to what had hit them and needed to make a few decisions that would help them bounce back. India was now going to play the Boxing Day test in Melbourne, where they had fond memories from back in 2018.

Second Test, Border-Gavaskar Trophy

Melbourne Cricket Ground, 26th December, 2020-30th December 2020

Australia was 1-0 up in the series, India was battered and bruised, and two of their main players were now not part of the series Virat Kohli and Mohammed Shami. India was looking depleted and under pressure.

Many pundits including Ricky Ponting, Adam Gilchrist, and Michael Vaughan were now anticipating a 4-0 whitewash for the Indians, their was so much hype around Virat Kohli that the Australian media had forgotten that other players also played for India.

Any optimistic Indian fan would have gone on to say that India has never lost a test match under Ajinkya Rahane's captaincy and there was a great chance of a comeback by the Indians.

In an interview Ravi Shastri just before the game said, it was a one-off game and the team has rubbed off to what has happened and is looking to write a new chapter in the rivalry.

Was India going to make changes for the coming test match, a couple of changes were anticipated with a couple of debuts lined up for the Indian team, and it was highly anticipated that Rishabh Pant and Ravindra Jadeja would also make a comeback into the team.

On the eve of the game that is Christmas Day India announced their team and they handed debuts two Shubman Gill and Mohammed Siraj. Wridhimann Saha and Prithvi Shaw were dropped from the team they were replaced by Rishabh Pant and Ravindra Jadeja. India had strengthened their middle order by bringing in Jadeja and Pant and had also strengthened their bowling as now India had 5 full-time bowlers. Some talks suggested that KL Rahul get a look in the team instead as he could provide stability in the middle but both Jadeja and Pant gave an additional benefit to the batting lineup by batting left-handed

Australia on the other hand didn't make any changes to their team and continued to play with the same team as they were extremely confident and knew they could put pressure on this depleted Indian team. But there is a rule, you never underestimate the Indian cricket team, when their backs are towards the wall that is the time this team is the most dangerous.

Playing XI

India: Mayank Agarwal, Shubman Gill, Cheteshwar Pujara, Ajinkya Rahane, Hanuma Vihari, Rishabh Pant, Ravindra Jadeja, Ravichandran Ashwin, Umesh Yadav, Jasprit Bumrah, Mohammed Siraj

Australia: Matthew Wade, Joe Burns, Marnus Labuschagne, Steven Smith, Travis Head, Cameron Green, Tim Paine, Pat Cummins, Mitchell Starc, Nathan Lyon, Josh Hazlewood

To perform well in this test India had to forget what happened in Adelaide and had to perform well in Melbourne this was India's best chance as India's record in Melbourne was something which India could be proud of and they knew that the conditions at the MCG is quite similar to those conditions in India.

DAY 1

Australian captain Tim Paine won the toss and without any hesitation decided to bat first knowing if the first hour of the first day is seen through without any harm they could dictate terms on India and push them to the wall.

The Indians knew that they needed early wickets and the only way to get them was by going full throttle with Jasprit Bumrah, Umesh Yadav, and Ravichandran Ashwin. It was important for India to make early inroads and force the Aussies to make mistakes.

Matthew Wade and Joe Burns came to open for Australia and this time India had a new opening bowling pair, Jasprit Bumrah and Umesh Yadav. The pressure had to be maintained from India's side and as they India didn't leave any page unturned and bowled in the right areas during the first hour of play.

They made sure Wade and Burns made some mistakes and gave away their wickets to the Indians and Bumrah just did the same and gave India the perfect start as Joe Burns knicked one to Rishabh Pant who took a simple catch and Burns had to depart for a 10 ball- duck.

There was a surprise sprung by India's captain Ajinkya Rahane in the first hour of play he introduced India's lethal weapon and that was Ravichandran Ashwin. Rahane had read the pitch perfectly and had understood that the pitch would grip for the spinners and even if Matthew Wade who was looking to attack the pacers might just look to attack the spinner and would give away his wicket.

Rahane's gut was extremely accurate and the same thing happened Wade tried to heave one in the leg side and got a top edge which just stood in the air, the drama had just begun. Gill was running from mid-wicket and Jadeja ran from his left from mid-on, there was confusion and the debutant was going to collide with the experienced campaigner. Jadeja the best fielder of the current generation didn't miss the chance and completed the catch. Wade had fallen into Ashwin's trap.

Ashwin who is an engineer by education had engineered one of the finest wickets and had given India the upper hand in the game. But Ashwin was just getting started, he was in no mood to put loosen the screws, and a beauty from the Chennai-lad, and a shrewd field placement by India captain Ajinkya Rahane saw the end of Steven Smith as the world's best test batter was gone caught in leg slip for a duck. India was ruling the game, it was a spirited fight from the Indians, it felt like the Indians had forgotten about the debacle at Adelaide and India was doing everything in their command to come on level terms with the Aussies.

Travis Head had joined Marnus Labuschagne, it was a chance for the Indian captain to introduce the debutant Mohammed Siraj to have a burst at the Australian middle -order but Rahane held back the debutant and only gave him an over during the dying minutes of the first session.

Siraj had started his spell on a defensive note but with every ball, he was gaining the confidence and the senior members of the team were giving him the motivation he wanted, there was a lot of hooting and noise of support for Siraj. Siraj who had lost his father a few weeks back had stayed back because of the COVID protocols and knew that he had a big task to complete and wanted to fulfill his dad's wish of becoming a top cricketer.

The partnership between Labuschagne and Head was getting momentum but in came Jasprit Bumrah who closed the day for Travis Head by bowling him short of length just outside off, which Head looked to push but took the edge and was cleanly taken by Rahane at gully. Travis Head was gone for 38 and Australia was reeling for 124/4.

Rahane knew India had a sniff and needed to capitalize on this and a couple of wickets would give India the perfect opportunity to get the early lead they wanted in the test match.

Rahane brought back Mohammed Siraj for a small burst at Labuschagne and Green, and Siraj didn't disappoint his captain. Ajinkya had placed Shubman Gill at backward square leg and had asked Siraj to ball from wide of the crease and get the ball to drift into the pads of the batter, and the plan worked straight away and Siraj got his first test wicket. The plan had worked India had pushed Australia to the wall and it was a big opportunity to finish the Australians for less than 200.

There was a controversial run-out which was supposedly given not-out in favor of the Aussie Captain Tim Paine. It was a very close call as Paine's bat appeared to be on the line of the crease when Rishabh knocked off the bails, the umpire didn't have conclusive evidence hence giving the decision in favour of the batter. Paine had received a life on 6 but Ashwin took care of him and got him for 13.

A little resistance from Nathan Lyon saw the score reach 195, with Jasprit Bumrah being the pick of the bowlers by picking 4 wickets. India had completed the first task but other things had to be completed, which would help India get back on level terms with Australia.

With just 11 overs remaining to play in the day, the two Indian openers had come to bat one was the experienced Mayank Agarwal who had made his test debut on the same ground in the last tour and the other was the Punjab-born young star, Shubman Gill. There were a lot of talks about Gill and his skillsets, everyone you knew would appreciate Gill and be in favor of him playing from the first test match in Adelaide.

India was once again off to a bad start a start which would give all their fans a mini-heart attack as Mayank was struck on the pads in the very first over and was adjudged LBW. Starc had given India another first-over shocker and India found themselves a wicket down without ticking the scorers.

But Shubman Gill was in a different mood and wanted to prove everyone right who had backed him, Gill played some beautiful shots, hit a couple of boundaries of Starc and Hazlewood, and some shots made everyone sit uptight on their sofas just to witness a new talent which was brewing in front of their eyes.

Everyone was excited as India ended the day on 36/1, with Gill unbeaten on 28 and Pujara unbeaten on 7. India were looking good and were hoping for a big lead by the end of Day 2.

DAY 2

India was ready for day 2, with an overnight score of 36/1. Debutant Gill and Pujara were all set to come and bat in conditions that were expected to be exploited by the Australian bowlers and the trio of Hazlewood, Starc, and Cummins.

Shubman was on an overnight score of 28 and I told my mom that this guy could make a good score in his debut game and could be one of those Indian cricketers to score a century in his debut test match, I was hoping for him to make a direct impact and score big in his first test innings.

Shubman didn't disappoint me and his fans as the youngster started extremely well he punished the bad balls and played some beautiful shots en route to his 45 before knicking a ball off Pat

Cummins to the wicketkeeper Tim Paine, Cheteshwar Pujara soon followed and India was struggling a bit at 64/3.

Then came Captain Ajinkya Rahane and Hanuma Vihari joined hands and knew they had a big task on their hands and had to play extremely well to take India to safety and see the team take a first-innings lead.

Ajinkya Rahane who was touring Australia for the third time had good memories of playing at MCG, he had scored a brilliant hundred at the G in his first series Down Under, where he had a beautiful partnership with Virat Kohli. This time around he had to not only build the innings but also build a partnership and also lead the team by example.

Rahane and Vihari looked steady against the bowlers and were looking to negate the pacers and the Aussie Spinner Nathan Lyon to get into a steady position. Both the batters known for their prowess in test cricket played with extreme caution and looked to take the game upon themselves and secure the game for the Indians.

Vihari was looking extremely confident against pace, but he was extremely tentative against the spin of Lyon, he was looking to play all kinds of shots against them and wasn't able to get under the pressure off his shoulder, eventually, he was dismissed by Lyon, to whom he was looking to play a sweep but the ball caught the back of the gloves and he was caught at slips by Steven Smith.

India was 116/4, and to join Ajinkya Rahane came the swashbuckling, fearless wicketkeeper Rishabh Pant. Rishabh was dropped from the limited overs team and was asked to concentrate on the test matches, he was asked to lose his recklessness to which he had lost his wicket in the last few months.

But to Rishabh's defense, he had an extremely good record against Australia in test cricket as he was the only 2nd cricketer to reach 25 in every against Australia in a record 8 innings. The first to achieve this was Sir Viv Richards for the mighty West Indies.

Rahane, on the other hand, was playing extremely sensibly taking singles and hitting the odd boundaries, he had left it to Rishabh to take the risk and tilt the game in India's favor, Rishabh was looking extremely confident in difficult situations and hit the ball extremely hard, the conditions were tough in Melbourne it was overcast for some time and there was moisture in the air which was helping the ball to move a little, to India's defense thankfully it was not the pink ball and it wasn't Adelaide.

India looked steady as the partnership between Rahane and Pant had crossed 50 runs and it came in just 73 balls, which was extremely quick. Rishabh Pant with his attacking cricket had taken out the condition and the Australian bowling out of the play, he had half-done the job and it was fair to say that Rishabh had unsettled the Australian bowling and India was on course to take a lead, and hopefully, a lead which would pressure on the Australian batters.

Mitchell Starc took his 250th test wicket in the form of Rishabh Pant as the left-hander looked to hit one over point but got a faint knick on the way to the keeper. Pant had fallen for a quick-fire 29 off just 40 balls. He had ensured that India was on the course to get a first-innings lead

To join Rahane who was slowly and steadily piling up his runs, came India's most trusted all-rounder Ravindra Jadeja, Jadeja joined hands with his captain and knew what was at stake. To nobody's surprise, both of them batted sensibly, and the best thing they did was they upped the ante and the run rate.

Rahane reached his 50, he was batting with utmost responsibility, and slowly India got the first innings they were looking for, now India was targeting a big lead a lead which would sweat the Aussie batters.

There was a small break in the proceedings because of the rain, and there was an extended tea, but after the extended break batting conditions became a little easier and both the batters took advantage of the conditions, India was finding their groove, and just after the tea they took the lead and the score reached 200.

Jadeja was complementing Rahane extremely well and to that the Australian bowlers had started to ball on a length which was helping the Indians get freebies and the bowlers were bowling extras which helped the Indians to relax a little and get the free runs.

Rahane had got the license and the Indian captain was now going behind the Australian bowling, suddenly after the rain break the pitch had become easier to bat on, and the batters were now able to rotate the strike very easily.

The two were looking secure and playing with confidence as India reached 250 and Rahane was closing on a beautiful ton at his favorite hunting ground. The India captain was not only mending for what had happened in Adelaide but was also giving a statement that India is not a pushover and the people who were talking about the clean sweep and nonsense, India would give a tough fight, they would either win or die trying.

Rahane was freely scoring runs of both Cummins and Hazlewood who were bowling in tandem, it felt like the man had understood the job role and was making the batting look extremely easy.

Rahane was at 96 when Cummins came to bowl in the last stages of the day, Rahane cut one fiercely to the backward point boundary, to get his 12th Test Century, 2nd at MCG, and a century which he would remember for a long time.

Rahane's century came at a situation when India was low on confidence, the captain had pumped new air into the team after scoring the century, he removed his helmet waved the bat to the dugout, and just said come on. No extravagant celebration, just clear focus and understanding of the game that a big task is at stake.

India ended the day at 277/5, the lead was almost 90 runs and India was hoping to extend the lead and demolish Australia on day 3. Rahane remained unbeaten on 104 and Ravindra Jadeja remained unbeaten on 40.

DAY 3

After a successful Day 2, the onus was on the Indians to start auspiciously on Day 3. To a certain extent, India started well playing on merit and getting the runs, and to the advantage of the batters the conditions had become better, and the ball was coming onto the bat and India was looking to get a big first-innings lead.

But confusion between Rahane and Jadeja had led to Rahane's first-ever dismissal by run-out, and after his dismissal, it was Jadeja who had to hold the Indian baton and en route to get that done, the Indian all-rounder scored a brilliant 50, and came out the sword celebration. He had played a fantastic knock, played a perfect second fiddle to Ajinkya Rahane, and saw that there was no collapse from his end.

But as the India tail was known to lose its way easily, the same thing happened and India was bundled out for 326. India had taken a considerable lead of 131 runs. It was now onto the bowlers to exploit the Aussie batters with the new ball and the conditions.

The two Australian openers Mathew Wade and Joe Burns came out to bat and were greeted with hostile bowling and were given nothing on offer, Joe Burns wasn't comfortable in the middle and it was seen that the opener was not able to get bat on ball and was facing difficulty facing both Bumrah and Umesh upfront.

Umesh Yadav who remained wicketless in the first innings took the first wicket and Joe Burns was adjudged out LBW. Umesh Yadav was pumped and he was looking all set to give a good fight to the Australian batters, but something happened that the Indian captain and camp were not hoping to happen.

Umesh was looking in good touch and was bowling at a fantastic speed was in his 4th over when the man pulled his hamstring, Umesh stopped and lay on the ground, he was not looking good and the Indians had now started to pray, the Indians were already without Ishant Sharma and now Mohammed Shami and Umesh Yadav were injured. Umesh Yadav was taken out of the ground and was ruled out of the test and test series. Siraj had to complete his over and put in the extra hard yard to make a memorable test match.

Indians were bowling extremely well and were not giving any room to the Australians, they had cramped the Australians, and with Ashwin coming into the attack it was going to be difficult for the Aussies to score runs, and the pressure got to Marnus Labuschagne and the Indian spinner got the wicket that the Indians were looking for as Ashwin found the outside edge of Labuschagne's bat and it was a simple catch for Ajinkya at slips.

Steve Smith soon followed as he was bowled down the leg by Jasprit Bumrah with a beauty of a ball, India was now bossing the game as the spinners had come into the attack and were taking wickets at regular intervals. Mohammed Siraj now was in the wicket column as he took the wicket of Travis Head as he nicked one to the second slip where Mayank Agarwal took a beautiful catch. India was bossing the game, and Australia was reduced to 98/5.

Green and Captain Tim Paine were in the middle as it had now become a difficult situation for the Australians as they were still some runs behind and India was looking good to wrap up the tail and get the victory by an innings.

This Indian lineup was extremely enthusiastic and was not going to leave any stone unturned to win the test match, they got the wicket of Tim Paine and Australia was 99/6. Cameron Green and Pat Cummins tried to rebuild the innings and played as many as balls possible only punishing the bad balls, both Green and Cummins batted till the end of the day and took the Australian score to 133/6, giving them a lead of 2 runs.

The inability of the Indian bowlers to bowl out a tail was seen once again, The Indian fans were hopeful of a win by an innings but they had to wake up again early in the morning and watch their team win or be hopeful of a win against the Aussies.

DAY 4

With an overnight score of 133/6, Australia was planning to get a lead of more than 100 so that they could get to India and try to get a few early wickets so the game could come in their favor.

Bumrah and Siraj started the proceedings for India and they were extremely good with their lengths and were testing the Australian batters, Green was trying to defend and get the singles and doubles so that the Indian team could get under pressure and commit mistakes but the patience and perseverance of the Indian bowlers and they hit the lines and lengths were not only helping them but was yielding a few results as there were a few DRS decisions which didn't go in their favor but was putting pressure on the Australian batters.

Bumrah with his consistency got the wicket of Pat Cummins and soon Siraj took the wicket of both Lyon and Green. Green who made his debut in the Adelaide test had shown why was he called Wonderboy and batted extremely well for his 45, to put pressure on the Indian team.

The pair of Starc and Cummins stayed together to put pressure on the Indians but the Indian bowlers and especially Ashwin held his line and lengths and took the all-important last wicket of Josh Hazlewood as the Australians were bundled out for 200.

Now it has to be understood that the pitch had become good for batting and it is said that while Ravichandran Ashwin was bowling, Shubman Gill came to him and said "Bhaiya, bowl them out for 50 and I shall chase this total in less than 5 overs"

This not only showed the confidence of a young batter but also showed how well Gill understood the situation and his reading of the game was extremely prompt. This was a sign of greatness that the young batter had.

There was also a fascinating fact that India had not let Australia score more than 200, in any of the innings they batted. This showed how potent the bowling was.

India only needed 70 to win the game and level the series at 1 game apiece before going into the New Year holidays and to Sydney.

Shubman opened the innings once again with Mayank and as promised he came out all guns blazing playing some beautiful shots through the on side and off side, played a couple of beautiful drives down the ground, and also played a beautiful drive down the ground.

Mayank and Cheteshwar Pujara fell to Starc and Cummins in consecutive overs which gave the Indian fans a little bit of a hiccup but the Indian Captain and Shubman Gill were determined not to lose any more wickets on the batting beauty and complete the run chase as quickly as possible.

Rahane who scored a brilliant century hit the winning runs for India by playing the ball towards the fielder at backward square leg which not only buried the ghosts of Adelaide but also gave India a win at Melbourne, this was the second time on the trot in two tours that India had won test matches at Melbourne.

There was rejuvenation in the Indian camp, there was happiness and also a sense of relief for the Indian supporters and players. This Indian team was looking to fight, this team was looking to perform extremely well in difficult situations, and as they say when the backs are towards the wall that is the time India is extremely dangerous.

Ajinkya Rahane was awarded the first-ever Mullagh Medal after being adjudged the Man of the Match. The captain had led the team front making exceptional bowling changes and doing some brilliant field placements not to take away anything from him in the way the man led the team.

For the next test match in Sydney, there was going to be the addition of the attacking, explosive opener Rohit Sharma, and another debut for an Indian bowler was lined up. India was hoping that there wouldn't be any other injury concerns but just after the game KL Rahul got injured and was released from the team, Shardul Thakur was called in as a cover in case of any other injuries, and Washington Sundar, Shreyas Iyer, T Natarajan, and Kartik Tyagi were asked to stay with the Indian team in case of any other mishaps.

3rd Test, Border Gavaskar Trophy

Sydney Cricket Ground, 7th January 2021- 11th January, 2021

The world had entered a new decade, It was the year 2021. The world has faced a deadly virus named COVID-19, lost their closed ones, and faced financial, mental, and physical losses. The only thing which gave people a sense of relief was the sport, in tough times. Cricket was a sport that gave the Indians a sense of self-belief and relief when they saw their country take on Australia early in the morning fighting to win and for self-respect away from all the criticism and take the challenge head-on and show them that they were the best cricketing nation in the world.

India was boosted with the addition of batting prowess Rohit Sharma, whose quarantine was over a couple of days after the Melbourne game, He had a chance to enjoy the new year with his team-mates and got an opportunity to get a hit and get the feel of the Australian conditions, Rohit who was a middle order batter in the test circuit had started to open for India in the test format, in 2019 during the home test series against South Africa and got results straight away. Rohit in that series scored 3 centuries which also included a double hundred in Ranchi. I was covering that test match in Ranchi, and believe me, the way Rohit was playing the South African bowling attack it felt like he was in a different zone, and opening batting in test cricket was just made for him.

On the other hand, India was thinking of whom to play in place of Umesh Yadav, there were two options that India had one of them being Navdeep Saini who if given a chance in the third test, would be making his test debut and the other option was Shardul Thakur, who had made his Test debut against West Indies in 2018 but had only bowled 8 balls before getting injured after pulling a groin muscle.

There were a few selection headaches for Ravi Shastri and Co, but as the great man had once said, Chill Karo, Sab Ho Jaayega. Ravi Shastri knew how to handle these situations and was sure enough to get a solution, assessing the pitch and conditions the Indians went ahead and decided to give a debut to Navdeep Saini.

But the concern was the same in the Aussie camp, Travis Head was not up to the mark and Joe Burns was injured, with David Warner coming back, the opening conundrum for Australia was all set to be solved as David Warner set to play the game and Will Pucosvki was set to replace Joe Burns.

Playing XI

India: Rohit Sharma, Shubman Gill, Cheteshwar Pujara, Ajinkya Rahane, Hanuma Vihari, Rishabh Pant, Ravindra Jadeja, Ravichandran Ashwin, Jasprit Bumrah, Mohammed Siraj, Navdeep Saini.

Australia: Will Pucovski, David Warner, Marnus Labuschagne, Steven Smith, Matthew Wade, Cameron Green, Tim Paine, Mitchell Starc, Pat Cummins, Nathan Lyon, Josh Hazlewood.

The teams announced by both India and Australia were on expected lines, with the series online both the teams knew a win in this would prove vital as the next test was going to be played in Gabba, Brisbane, a ground where Australia had last lost to the mighty West Indies in 1988.

DAY 1

The stage was set for both the teams, and it was going to be a cracker jacker of a test, the last time both the teams played in Sydney in 2019, India had a fantastic outing, Pujara and Pant scored a fantastic century, Pujara had agonizingly fell short of his double century, and the rain had spoilt India's plan of winning the series 3-1.

This time around India was playing with a different captain, a slightly different team but the energy was high, and you could feel it during the toss when Tim Paine had elected to bat after winning the toss. Ajinkya Rahane said that we would exploit the condition and bowl in the right areas to put the Australians on the back foot.

India was pumped and you could see it on the face of the Indian cricketers as well during the National Anthem when the players looked determined with every word of Jana Gana Man being played at the historic SCG, the demeanour of the Indian players was growing. Mohammed Siraj who was playing his second test match was seen a little emotional, Jasprit Bumrah was standing beside him during the Anthem and was seen consoling him after the anthem was done.

His father would have been proud seeing his son, making India proud and playing for India at the highest level.

The game had started and India opened the bowling with their heroes of the previous game Jasprit Bumrah and Mohammed Siraj, India was looking to exploit conditions and get the best out of the pitch, but it is important to know that the pitch at SCG is historically known to be helpful for the batters, it is known to yield big runs.

India attacked the comeback man David Warner as he was coming back after a big lay-off and Siraj was the wrecker in chief he continuously bowled difficult questions and immediately it yielded results as Warner tried reaching to a full ball which took the outside edge and Cheteshwar Pujara who was standing in slips took an easy catch. India was on top and the new pace bowling sensation was taking wickets for India straight away. India looked to put pressure on Pucovski and Labuschagne and the questions that were being asked were extremely difficult as both the ball was passing their outside edge and there was nothing given on offer to the Australian batters.

The rain had interrupted the game and an early lunch was taken and the weather was looking inclement for cricket to happen, Australia's score was 21/1 at lunch with only 7 overs being bowled. The rain had stayed for a long time and the outfield was getting sluggish. This meant that the ground staff would need more time to get the game to start, as they needed to remove water from the outfield and make it playable.

The match restarted in the 2nd Session and the conditions became better to bat as the ball was now coming to the bat and the Australians were now getting the runs easily, the runs had started to flow slowly and steadily the partnership reached 50, and then Will Pucovski reached his 50, India needed a wicket otherwise given the history and the conditions it felt like the Australians would run away with the game, and Rahane then turned to his debutant Navdeep Saini, who had been given the task of removing another debutant Will Pucovski, and Saini didn't disappoint his captain as a full ball with pace had found the opener in front of the stumps and was adjudged out.

It was a fantastic start to his international test career as Will Pucovski's first Innings in international cricket came to an end at 62.

Steve Smith walked to bat, the best test batter didn't have a memorable two test matches and had a point to prove in front of his home crowd, it was going to be important for him to play and get the nerves away. Also, the form of Smith was concerning for the Australian team as the Aussies had not scored more than 200, in any of the 4 innings they had batted in the first two test matches. It was Smith who always took Australia on his shoulders, in the middle period of the game, the number of runs he was going to score was going to be the key for Australia as it would determine how much the Aussies would score in the first innings.

Marnus Labuschagne was continuing his form and scored yet another half-century as the young Aussie Batter reached 50, in just 108 balls which comprised of 6 beautiful boundaries.

Smith and Labuschagne played well and continued to put pressure as they batted till the end of the day to put up an unbeaten partnership of 60, to take the score to 166/2 at the end of play on Day 1.

India had done extremely well in controlling the flow of runs, but the Australian batters looked undisturbed with whatever came their way, It was going to be important for the Indian bowlers to take wickets at the start of the day's play otherwise Australia had the ammunition to run away with the game. The first session of Day 2 was going to be important for the Indians, and could well set the tone of the test match at Sydney.

DAY 2

Australia was looking to score big and it wouldn't be a surprise as their two best batters were out in the middle and were playing on merit and were looking extremely good, the weather was still a little gloomy and the weather prediction was showing that there would be rain in the early parts of the day and could play spoilsport during the first session of play.

India, on the other hand, was looking for wickets, they needed early wickets and couldn't let Labuschagne or Steve Smith settle, because they knew if those two settled they would go for the kill and score big which could put unnecessary pressure on the Indians to chase a big 4th Innings total and could even throw India out of the test match.

Smith and Labuschagne both started on a good note, they were getting the runs easily and were able to score without any pressure from the Indian bowlers, the Indian bowlers were not getting anything from the surface and they were able to put pressure on the Indian contingent.

The rain was causing an interruption in the play but the rains were not as hard as it was on Day 1, there were a couple of passing showers which led to a stoppage in play.

The rains and continuous interruption didn't lead to any blockage or brain fade in the batters as they were going by their jobs with ease and batting without much issue, Marnu Labuschagne looked in brilliant touch and the way he was knocking the balls all over the crowd was extremely beautiful, he was playing attacking cricket, which made Rahane introduce spin from both the ends as there was a little purchase for the spinners from the pitch.

Jadeja was bowling extremely tight lines and was able to get the ball to turn, many including me were thinking that a wicket was around the corner but both the premier Australian batters were looking in the zone hitting the odd bad ball for runs and boundaries. India needed a wicket desperately the batters were looking comfortable batting and were looking to take away the game, they had put up a hundred partnership and were looking to build on that. But the partnership breaker Ravindra Jadeja did what he was known to do, bowling on the right lines and lengths, getting the ball to turn and bounce, getting the outside edge of Marnus Labuschagne's bat and Rahane who had positioned himself at first slip took a very alert catch, low to his right.

India had got the opening they wanted, and then Captain Rahane turned to his best bowler and was hoping that he could crack the Aussie middle order. Jasprit Bumrah didn't disappoint his captain, as Bumrah along with Jadeja spun the web and got the wickets of Wade, Green, Paine, and Cummins. The score which was looking to go past 400-450, was now 278/7, India was hoping to catch the Australians and get the restrict them as low as possible. But for that, they had to get one man by the name of Steven Smith.

Smith was off-color in the first two games as he was being mauled by Ashwin and Bumrah, there were memes and comparisons of his batting with India's Umesh Yadav who had scored more than him. During the new year break, Smith worked a little on his technique and how to counter Ashwin and Bumrah who were having his number in the test series so far.

Smith played a fine knock to shush the critics by scoring a beautiful century at his home ground and started the new year in prime fashion. He had found his mojo and he was now set, with wickets falling at the other end he had decided not to slow down and had decided to keep going without any fear and apprehensions. India was looking to close the innings as Australia had already reached 338 and anything more than 350, would have given the Aussies the mental and psychological lead.

But a fielding masterpiece brought the Australian innings to a close as a shot by Smith was played toward the square leg region and Jadeja sprinted from Deep Square leg to collect the ball and aim at the stumps as Smith was coming back for the second, and with Ravindra Jadeja and his rocket arm you don't take the risk of taking the second, and Jadeja didn't disappoint anyone as the rocket arm of Jadeja hit the stumps and Smith was caught out of the crease. India was ecstatic as they had bowled the Aussies for less than 350, and had given them a chance to get close to the score or even get a lead.

India needed to bat extremely well to get a good start and with Rohit back in the team, there were expectations of a terrific start from the Indian team. Shubman and Rohit Sharma came to open for India in Sydney, this was India's 6th opening pain in the last 6 test matches against Australia in Australia.

India was going to be tested against the Aussie pace battery but they needed to be careful and had to bat extremely well, Sharma an expert campaigner was opening for the first time in test cricket away from home. Shubman had shown signs of good batting in the Melbourne test where he batted with a calm head and played some exquisite shots.

India was off to a very decent start and had seen off the first part of the game and had played sensibly till tea and it was time that the Indians batted with extreme stability and sensibility so that they could get closer to the total.

Rohit had gotten into the groove he was pulling and getting the runs at ease, he took his time but once he settled in he got the runs at ease. Rohit's form was giving India the hope they wanted, but as they say, the promising things come to an anti-climatic end as Rohit chipped one back to Hazlewood as India lost their first wicket after a promising start.

On the other hand, Shubman Gill played some beautiful shots and was looking good with the bat in his hand, he went on to score his maiden half-century of his test career, and the future was truly bright for the baby GOAT. But as soon as he reached 50, he was caught by Cameron Green at Gully as India was reduced to 85/2.

Rahane and Pujara had joined hands together and had closed the shop for India, they were not looking to do anything extravagant, they were just bodying the ball or defending it. This approach of the captain and vice-captain was highly criticized and the Former India Captain and Legend Sunil Gavaskar mentioned that India was too meek in their approach and didn't have the guts to take the risk and put pressure on the Australians.

India ended the day at 96/2 with Pujara and Rahane ending the day at unbeaten 9 and 5 respectively. It was going to be a big day for India on Day 3 as it would set the tone for the result of the test match and the test match looked even stevens, with the game due on Day 3, the Sydney test was all set to get more interesting.

DAY 3

India was looking to build on the momentum they had created on Day 2 and wanted to continue the good batting performance that they had shown in Melbourne, India needed a level-headed approach for Day 3, the most important part of Day 3 was going to be how India was going to shape up as a team, their psychological understanding and level-headedness was going to be tested.

India started well with both Rahane and Pujara looking to score the runs in the early stage of the day and avoid making the same mistake that they had committed in the closing phases of the day.

A positive-looking Rahane and a positive-looking Pujara steadied the ship for India and were looking to take the Indian score to close to 200 when a beautiful ball from Pat Cummins got the inside edge of Rahane's bat and Rahane was bowled for 22.

Pujara on the other hand was taking his time playing his shots and was doing what he does more often occupy the pitch and irritate and tire the Australians. But the Australian bowlers were bowling on the right areas and were successful in taking the wickets of Hanuma Vihari, with which in came India's most fascinating batter, a batter who if batted for an hour could take the game away from the opposition.

Rishabh Pant needed to do everything right to take India to safety, and Rishabh being Rishabh, didn't loosen the nozzle but rather started attacking from ball 1, he was batting with Pujara, one being the aggressor and the other being calm as an cucumber.

Rishabh was playing the sheer aggressor's role and was striking the ball well, but something unprecedented happened which caused a major setback in the Indian camp, the Indian team was already plagued with injuries as Shami, Umesh Yadav, and KL Rahul were already back home owing injuries and Ishant Sharma was not selected because of an injury.

A ball from Pat Cummins which kept low hit Rishabh Pant on the hand and it was visible that the young wicketkeeper-batsman was in tremendous pain, Indian management was chewing their nails seeing the condition, Nitin Patel the Indian physio had come down to the center to check if everything was all right or not Pant was in severe pain but decided to continue and eventually got out for 36 as his wicket started a flurry of wickets for Australia and India were reduced to 206/7 with Pujara, Ashwin and Pant all 3 out in the span of 5 overs and 10 runs.

India was on the verge of giving away a big lead which could have caused a big issue for India as the Indian team could have been chasing a big total which could have been a problem for the Indian team. But the worst was about to come as Jadeja who was batting and trying to get closer to the first innings score made by Australia. Starc was steaming in and was bowling extremely well when one ball hit Jadeja on the left thumb and there was speculation of Jadeja dislocating his left thumb, which to some extent was understood to be true. Nitin Patel had a big job ahead, he needed to keep the players ready and was going to be on his toes for the rest of the game.

India was bundled out for 244, giving Australia a lead of 94. Australia had taken a big first-innings lead and the pressure was on India now, the pendulum had shifted toward Australia and the Indians had to be ready to chase a steep total.

Early tea was taken and the Indians had some problems to address as Rishabh and Jadeja both were taken for scans which meant Saha had to keep in his place and India was a bowler short. Jadeja had bowled extremely well in the first innings and was the live wire in the field.

Australia came and was a little tentative, both Warner and Pucovski were tentative against both Bumrah and Siraj where Siraj brokethrough the opening pair and got the first wicket and then Ashwin joined the party by taking the wicket of David Warner.

The trusted partnership of Smith and Labuschagne made sure that Australia didn't lose another wicket and saw the Aussies to safety at the end of day play. India had bowled extremely well in the second innings but the batting sense shown by the Australians eluded India from the wicket. Australia now had a lead of 197, India needed a moment of magic to get a target that could be realistically chased.

DAY 4

At the end of Day 3, something unwanted and unprecedented occurred as the Indian pacers Jasprit Bumrah and Mohammed Siraj complained to the umpires about racial abuses that they had received from the crowd, there was a lengthy conversation with umpires Paul Wilson and Paul Reiffel in the dressing room, where the captain

Rahane and Coach Ravi Shastri and David Boon who was the match referee for the 3rd test in Sydney.

Siraj who was fielding at the Randwick end of the ground, when he was fielding at fine leg had heard of some racial slurs, the officials talked to both Bumrah and Siraj. Cricket Australia was looking into the case and stated the issue as inappropriate behavior.

At the start of Day 4, India needed to get early wickets and had to make sure that the Australians didn't run away with the game, the Indians needed to be careful and needed to get the early wickets, and Australia started on a good note and batted with extreme caution and didn't take unnecessary chances.

Saini made sure that Marnus Labuschagne didn't reach his hundred got the outside edge of the latter's bat and gave India the first wicket of the day. Saini didn't stop here he got the second wicket of the spell when Matthew Wade poked one to the substitute keeper Wriddhiman Saha and Australia was now in a little bit of trouble as Cameron Green joined the experienced campaigner Steven Smith.

Smith was looking good as he made a well-compiled 73 and reached another half-century of the test match, he had already shut the mouths of his critics and he was on a roll. Steven Smith had made a good partnership with Green and the partnership was now nearing 300, and it was going to be a dreaded target to chase for the Indians as the scan results of both Jadeja and Pant had come in which Pant's reports had come fine but Jadeja's result was not very good as the ace-allrounder had suffered from a dislocated thumb and was not going to ball for the remainder of the test match and batting looked a little uncertain.

What it meant was that India had suffered from another injury and now the question arose, who would replace him for the next test match?

Meanwhile, there was another unfortunate incident with Mohammed Siraj, which was brought to the notice of the umpires and the Indian captain Ajinkya Rahane and his counterpart Tim Paine, the racial slurs had begun once again, this time it was bad as other players such as Mayank Agarwal and Cheteshwar Pujara had also joined the discussion, it had become a big thing.

The game was stopped for some time, and the umpires, match referee David Boon, security staff, and Cricket Australia intervened. When the incident happened, Siraj went right to the umpire and told the umpire Paul Reiffel about the unprecedented incident that had occurred.

This time Indians had taken an aggressive role and decided to point out where the racial slurs were coming from, The umpires, and Australian players all were supportive of this decision and even asked the Indian captain to leave the ground if they wished to, Ajinkya Rahane famously said "We are here to play cricket and that is our main motive."

The security staff had identified the culprits and had asked four men to vacate the stadium and they were banned from entering the cricket ground.

Sean Carroll who was the head of the integrity and security for Cricket Australia, released a statement saying that Cricket Australia condemned the act strongly and hosts of the series between India and Australia showed their remorse.

After a 10-minute gap the game had restarted and the Indian team now needed a wicket as Australia was already closing on a target nearing 400.

Bumrah brought Cameron Green's innings to an end as the young Western Australian batter got out at 84 off just 132 balls. Australia decided to declare the innings and have a shot at bowling out India as they set them a target of 407.

India had 34 overs in the day to make a bold statement or to settle their nerves and then go for the chase on day 5, whereas the Australians were looking to take as many as wickets they could and put India in the backseat.

India wanted to continue their good momentum from the game in Melbourne and wanted to show the Aussies that they were no pushovers. The two Indian openers Rohit Sharma and Shubman Gill, came to open the innings for India, two batters who were opening for India for the first time but in the days to come would open more often and beautifully complement each other.

India needed 407 runs to win the test and had almost 131 overs to chase the daunting target, the Indian batters had to bat with extreme caution and understanding, lapse in concentration would have led to something extremely catastrophic.

It was also to be understood that Ravindra Jadeja had a dislocated thumb and would not be able to bat, or even if he came to bat he wouldn't be able to survive.

Rohit and Gill had a task on their hands, a partnership of around 130-150, would have tilted the game in India's favor, as India could win the game if the openers gave India the start they were looking for.

Rohit and Shubman saw the new ball, adjusted themselves on the pitch, and then looked to attack the pace trio of Starc, Hazlewood, and Cummins along with Nathan Lyon. Rohit Sharma was playing his favorite pull shot and piercing the field as it looked like a setting made in heaven for Rohit.

The conditions had gotten better for the batters and both the batters were looking to capitalize, the opening duo had put up a partnership of 50, and both of them were looking focused to help India reach close to the target.

When things were looking positive for India, a mishap and Shubman Gill was caught behind courtesy of a delivery from Josh Hazlewood, which had kissed the outside edge of Gill's bat and flown to the keeper Tim Paine.

India had lost their first wicket at the score of 71, Pujara joined Rohit and had only agenda to bat till the end of the day, without taking any risks but Rohit being Rohit, loved to take the risks and reached his 50.

As they say, the loved ones are the cause of your demise, in the same manner, Rohit's beloved pull shot was the cause of his dismissal as a short ball that had hit me written all over it and Rohit mistimed the ball and Starc at backward square leg took the catch and put a full stop to his innings.

India was now reeling at 92/2 and still had over 300 runs to chase, India needed a miracle and with just 4 overs remaining in the day, Captain Ajinkya Rahane came out to bat, the task was simple as both the batters now had to steady the ship rather than going for the big shots.

Former India captain Sunil Gavaskar had appreciated Rahane's bold move to come out to bat in the last stages of the game rather than sending a night watchman, according to the Indian legend he said that it was a very positive sign that the captain came at the end of the day which showed the eagerness of getting a favorable result.

India ended the day with 98/2, still needing 309 runs to win. It was a herculean task, and after the end of the day I said this to everyone, I hope we continue to bat by the time I am awake, that would be tending towards the end of the second session.

But deep down we all knew, we could trust this Indian team, India was going to make us proud. This team had what it took to be called champions.

DAY 5

With 309 to chase, India had a task on their shoulders, the two batters on the crease had to do something special to bring India close to the target.

Paine took the rabbit out of the hat and introduced Nathan Lyon early in the day, and to add to India's misery and Australia's happiness, he got the important wicket of India's captain and talisman Ajinkya Rahane, as Rahane played one straight to the hands of the fielder stationed at Short leg. India was in deep misery and was now looking at a heavy defeat.

India with their backs toward the wall, sent the wicket-keeper batter Rishabh Pant at 5 instead of Hanuma Vihari, who was batting at five after the Adelaide test and Kohli's return to India. It is said that, while Kohli was leaving for India he had a word with Head Coach Ravi Shastri and Batting Coach Vikram Rathour about the swashbuckling southpaw, and whether he would be a good fit at 5.

With India being in a tough situation and looking at Rishabh Pant's nature of taking the game away from the opposition, it was seen to be a wise choice. Pant joined hands with Pujara it felt like it was a mixture of fire and ice together.

Pant against a spinner was going to be some contest and Rishabh didn't disappoint, he came all guns blazing and was smashing Lyon all over the park, he was fearless but what was scaring the fans and the team management was Rishabh's ability to change from a fearless player to a reckless player. Everyone was praying and hoping that the young keeper would continue to attack.

Rishabh who scored a beautiful 150 at the same venue, during India's tour in 2018-19, had some beautiful memories and wanted to continue in the same way and manner to get the team close to victory.

On one hand, Rishabh was looking to attack the pacers, on the other Pujara was playing patiently without taking any risks, he was playing out maidens and leaving it on Pant to smash the bowlers. India was slowly and steadily building a partnership.

This knock which Rishabh was playing was going to be his coming of age, and a knock on the doors to be one of the all-time Indian greats.

Rishabh had already raced past to a fifty in just 64 balls which consisted of 4 boundaries and 3 brilliant sixes. India had reached the 200-run mark just at the stroke of lunch and India now needed only 201 runs to win this historic test.

Pujara was slowly and steadily reaching 50, Pujara had his task cut out he knew what had to be done, and was just standing in one place and occupying the crease and not giving it to the bowlers.

The middle session of the day was going to be important for India, India couldn't lose wickets and the fall of any wicket would mean India to be in deep trouble. A good 120-run session would mean India to be at the top of Australia and rule the game.

It was also important to understand the only batsman left after this pair was Hanuma Vihari, as Jadeja had a dislocated thumb and Ashwin the batter couldn't be relied on as much as Jadeja the batter.

Rishabh Pant had now raced to the 90s, he was batting on a different track and was batting with extreme usage of temperament, not taking too many risks but putting pressure on the Australians. Pant was reminded by the senior pro that he had reached his nervous nineties and had to play sensibly to get to that 100-figure mark, but Rishabh being Rishabh did what he knows the best tried to go for the big slog in the leg side by dancing down the ground, got the outside edge and was caught at gully by Pat Cummins.

Rishabh Pant was distraught by himself, he knew he had a big role to play in the run chase, by taking his wicket Australia was now back on top as the X-factor which India had perished.

Cheteshwar Pujara had reached his half-century in 170 balls, he was playing the sheet anchor role, and Hanuma Vihari had now come to the middle to support Cheteshwar Pujara.

The Indian scoring rate had now taken a hit, the runs weren't coming easy and it was very difficult for the Indians to score the runs easily the Australians had started to put the pressure on the Indian batters with short balls and toe-crushing yorkers, and the Indians needed a solution, India needed to do something, they needed a spark of belief.

But as soon as the Indians were starting to look to rebuild, the Indians were once again hit with an injury and this time it was to Hanuma Vihari who had pulled his hamstring and was not able to walk or run. The tension in the Indian camp was increasing, half of the Indian team was now injured and there was a little problem for the Indians now.

To add to India's misery Hazlewood got the wicket of Cheteshwar Pujara who was looking extremely good with the bat, was done with a ball that kept straight and didn't do much.

Now two of the three batters with some batting ability left were injured and it was famously quoted by Harsha Bhogle on the air that India now had 1 Man, 1 Hand, and 1 Leg left. It was being referred to Ashwin, Jadeja, and Vihari.

Ashwin joined Vihari on a tough pitch and if you saw the game closely you would have seen that even Ashwin was not completely comfortable with his lower back. India somehow managed to survive the last half-hour before tea.

India was now at 280/5 at the end of the second session, to win the test match India needed 127 runs to win in the remaining 36 overs, But did they have the gas and the ammunition left in the tank?

The last session was going to be a transpiring and interesting final session as the Indians needed 127 to win, the Australians needed 5 wickets and both the teams had 36 overs to do whatever they could.

The first ball of the tea had set the tone of what was going to happen in the last session of the third Sydney test. Pat Cummins was handed the ball by the captain Tim Paine, and the first ball was a short-pitched spicy bouncer that had taken the kissed the arm-guard and popped to the wicketkeeper.

The umpire had given it out, but Ashwin quickly reviewed and the DRS showed it had taken a part of the arm-guard on its way to the wicketkeeper. India was relieved, it was not going to be easy for the Indians, things were going to be difficult and it was to be understood that the trio of Hazlewood, Cummins, and Hazlewood were not going to relax against Ashwin and Vihari.

Jadeja who was padded up to come next was seen in pure discomfort as Navdeep Saini was helping him eat a banana and also helping him wear the gloves. The situation for the Indians was very tight, the two batters in the middle had to save the test match for India, both had cooked up a plan, they were not attacking the bowlers or looking for the runs, both were just looking to play each delivery on its merit and not do anything extravagant. India needed assurance, and it felt like with every ball being bowled both were assuring India that we are here, you don't need to worry.

Ashwin was feeling the pain in his back and it was evident also the visit of physio Nitin Patel had become extremely frequent as the Aussies were extremely hostile in their approach and were attacking the batters by bowling bodyline.

Hazlewood and Cummins were targeting Ashwin on his body and Ashwin just like a wall was defending, ducking, and taking the blows on the body. Ashwin was extremely strong in his mindset he knew Hanuma Vihari couldn't run, he had to hit the ball as far as possible so that Vihari could finish the run. Whoever was watching the game realized that if India couldn't win the game, they wouldn't let Australia also win the game.

With every passing ball and every passing over the voice and claps of Indian fans at SCG were getting better, the claps had started to come with every ball bowled and every ball defended.

Hanuma Vihari on the other hand didn't do anything special, if the ball was in the line of the stumps he was just defending it and if it was wide off the stumps or down the leg side he would just let it pass by.

Ravi Shastri on the other hand was sending Shardul Thakur at every interval to give the two instructions, but Shardul would go to the middle and Ashwin would ask him what the instructions were and the Mumbai lad would say I have forgotten what they told me to tell, you play the way you are playing.

The game was getting extremely tense and there was a lot of verbal talk, sledging, and pressure that was being applied on the Indian batters, there were a few catches that were dropped and it was seen that the Australians had come under the pump. Tim Paine was not able to think properly, and it was seen that the Indian cricket team had an upper hand over the Aussies. The two Indian batters were talking to each other between the overs in four different languages, Hindi, English, Tamil, and Telugu.

Ashwin and Vihari were now having fun, they were taking care of everything that was coming their way, an overly charged Starc was trying to dismantle the two but they stood in between the Aussies and a victory at Sydney.

The resilience that was shown by the two was remarkable, there was grit, there was pain and there was the love of the game and the passion they had for their country, what the two were doing was beyond imaginable, we as Indian fans were having a remarkable time.

I still remember when my best mate Goutam Choudhury was attending the finance class on Cisco Webex along with me and we were also discussing this particular game, he was telling me, one ball at a time and we can get the bloody draw, one ball at a time come on India.

A few overs were remaining for India to take away the draw a draw which would be remembered by every fan, with every passing ball the pressure and anxiety were increasing, I had started to count the number of balls that were remaining, it was becoming a good game and a memorable game, I could feel the excitement and the happiness. The only thing I hoped for was no other hiccups to happen and for India to take the game toward a draw smoothly.

The Australians had gotten irritated and it was visible, that Tim Paine who had missed a few catches was so irritated that he went on abusing Ravichandran Ashwin and said "We, will see you at Gabba".

The Australians were proud of their rich heritage at Gabba and as they called it Gabbatoir, as they had not lost a test match in Gabba for the last 32 years.

The Indians with the day's play coming to an end started to play their shots, Ashwin hit some boundaries as Captain Tim Paine and the batters shook hands with the umpire to announce the game as a draw.

India had pulled off a historic draw, Vihari who was injured faced 161 balls for his 23, and Ashwin faced 128 balls for his 39. India had done the unthinkable, the final day of the game was topsy-turvy. In the end, it was India who had snatched a satisfying draw and remained in the test series, making it clear that they were no pushovers.

The series now moved to Gabba for its fourth and final test match at the Gabba. India had a few issues which needed to be solved as Jadeja and Hanuma Vihari were injured and were already ruled out of the series.

In July 2023, I had an opportunity to meet Hanuma Vihari in Bangalore during the finals of the Deodhar Trophy had asked him what kept him going during the final stages of the game, and he smiled back at me and said only one thing, it was the love for my country which kept me going.

For India to breach Gabba they had to do something special, were the Indians able to do something special?

4th Test, Border Gavaskar Trophy

Gabba, Brisbane, 15th January 2021- 19th January, 2021

The stage was set, and India had arrived at Brisbane after pulling out the most dramatic draw ever known to anyone in mankind. As a cricket lover and fanatic, I hadn't seen something of this sort all my life, I had fallen in love with the idea of aggressive and attacking cricket and the resilience shown by the Indians. The Indians were looking to do something special as the Border-Gavaskar Trophy and a place in the finals of World Test Championship final was on stake.

But was it going to be easy, the Australian Captain had already warned Ashwin and had already invited the man to Gabba, Paine was sure of a victory and why shouldn't he have been confident about the victory? India was depleted, and Vihari and Jadeja were ruled out of the game owing to injuries and it was looking like India were going to make more changes as Ashwin and Bumrah were not a match fit.

Ashwin as told by his wife Prithi Narayan, was not able to bend his back and tie his shoelaces on the final day of the Sydney test and Jasprit Bumrah was suffering from a leg injury.

India now added Natarajan, Kartik Tyagi, and Washington Sundar to the team. A test match for Shardul Thakur was now looking inevitable, but who would play in the playing XI?

Rahane though confessed that he was so scared that when the team was coming onto the ground before the game, he was counting the number of players and was hoping that no one would get injured.

Sundar was a surety as there needed to be a like-for-like replacement for Ravindra Jadeja and Sundar was the only option available to India. Sundar was drafted into the team and the first thing they had to do was get kits for him and they had to buy pads from a local sports shop.

Guess what happened next, the Indian team manager had to go to a local sports shop in Brisbane to get a pair of pads for him, Sundar who is the tallest in the group was not able to fit in anybody else's pads hence needed a new pair of white pads.

India was down and out on resources and on the number of players they had. The other question was who would replace Hanuma Vihari, India had a few options, and they went in with Mayank Agarwal. The best thing about this selection was Mayank knew how to bat in the middle order, and if he batted when the second new ball was taken, he had the experience to play through the tough phase and could also provide stability to the team.

For Australia to win the Border Gavaskar Trophy they had to win the 4th and final test and for India to retain the trophy they either needed to play a draw or win the test. India's head coach had instilled the belief in the team that they knew they could do it the Indians were pumped they knew they had a task on their hands and they knew if they had to pull the rabbit out of their hats, they needed to play out of their skins.

India had not announced the team a day before and there were rumors that India didn't have 11 fit players to play the game. But the real reason was they were still waiting for an update on Jasprit Bumrah as his availability would have boosted the Indian team, beautifully.

On the other hand, Australians were going with the same team apart from the change where Marcus Harris was going to replace Will Pucovski, who was not fit for the game.

Playing XI:

India: Rohit Sharma, Shubman Gill, Cheteshwar Pujara, Ajinkya Rahane, Rishabh Pant, Mayank Agarwal, Washington Sundar, Shardul Thakur, Navdeep Saini, Mohammed Siraj, T Natarajan

Australia: David Warner, Marcus Harris, Marnus Labuschagne, Steven Smith, Matthew Wade, Cameron Green, Tim Paine, Pat Cummins, Mitchell Starc, Nathan Lyon, Josh Hazlewood

DAY 1

India was depleted, the only two players who had played all four test matches were Rahane and Pujara. Both played immense roles in India's resurgence, and the way they played showed a path for the Indians.

The Indian bowling looked extremely weak it felt as if India was playing an A game or a tour game, Two debutants, Sundar and Natarajan. Saini and Thakur were playing their 2nd test match and even in that Shardul had only bowled a handful of balls. The senior bowler India had was none other than Mohammed Siraj, who had only played 2 test matches before this test.

It was an overhaul for the Indians, No Kohli, Jadeja, Ashwin, Vihari, Bumrah, Shami, Ishant, and Umesh. As an average fan, you would think how on earth will these boys win, it is impossible to win. But deep down everyone had the trust that anyone who could pull off a miracle was going to be India.

The debut caps were handed, and it had come to a stage where people were talking about India not playing the game because they didn't have an 11 to play with.

But to India's fighting spirit, India came to play, the toss happened, and Australia once again was batting first. It was going to be difficult for the India new ball bowlers. Without Jasprit Bumrah the bowling attack was looking toothless, it was going to be a game of the spirits India needed to show that they had an unwavering and unbreakable spirit and would give the Aussies a tough time.

As Tim Piane had said on the final day of the Sydney Test " See you at Gabba", and here we were at Gabba, only time could tell us if Tim Paine would smile at the statement, or have a wry smile, kicking himself for telling that to Ravi Ashwin.

Marcus Harris opened the innings with David Warner, Australia had a good opportunity to put pressure on the Indians, Mohammed Siraj who was in his 3rd test was leading this bowling unit, he opened the bowling for India and the man didn't disappoint, he was right on the mark. He was bowling in the right areas from ball 1.

Siraj in his first over was extremely consistent with his line and was rewarded on the last ball of the 1st over of the test, Warner played an uncertain shot and got an edge which flew to the slips and was taken beautifully by Rohit Sharma who dived to his right. India had got the start they wanted the Indians were ecstatic. India got a wicket in the very first over of the test and for a moment it felt like a wicket here or there and India could dominate the Aussies.

To support Siraj, Natarajan opened the bowling for India. Natarajan who had made his international debut in ODI just 45 days back, went on to make his debut for India in all three formats on this tour and became the first Indian to make his debut in all three formats on the same tour.

Natarajan the left-handed fast bowler had picked the lengths quickly and it was going to be extremely important to see how Rahane would use him throughout the test match.

Rahane was proactive with his captaincy and as he saw some movement on the ball he brought in Shardul Thakur, Shardul who had played only bowled 10 balls in test cricket before this test match was ready to make an impact straightaway. The first ball he bowled on his return to test cricket, he got the wicket of Marcus Harris. The ball was on the pads of Harris and he flicked it straight to Washington Sundar who was stationed at square leg.

Australia was now reeling on 17/2 when the two best batters of the Sydney Test got together to make a good case for the team and take the Aussies out of the soup it was going to be very important to see how these two play in front of a pumped India bowling attack who had nothing to lose.

Labuschagne who was playing in front of his home crowd had a point to prove and wanted to get his first century against India after narrowly missing out in the Sydney test, both Labuschagne and the senior pro-Steve Smith started the repair work but didn't bother to play difficult balls and just took singles whenever possible and hit the boundaries on odd bad bowls.

The two took Australia to safety till lunch as Australia ended the first session at 65/2, Labuschagne and Smith both showed character and weren't doing anything stupid as the Indians were now over them.

After the lunch break, India immediately brought on Washington Sundar and it was worth in gold as Smith's weakness against off-spin was exposed and the experienced campaigner flicked one to Rohit Sharma who was standing at short mid-wicket, India had brought the Australians under pressure but until Labuschagne was there, it was not going to be easy for the Indians, a good partnership between Labuschagne and Wade or any other middle order batter would cause stress and tension in the Indian camp.

Wade joined hands with Marnus Labuschagne to start Australia's resurgence in the test math. Rahane on the other hand was switching his bowlers beautifully, he was not letting Australians settle as he was rotating the four fast bowlers and Washington Sundar beautifully.

But as everything was going well, Navdeep Saini who was playing his 2nd test match and who was bowling his 8th over got a side strain and once again India was a bowler short, with Rahane looking to use Natarajan with the old ball, he was forced to use him in the middle session.

Meanwhile slowly and steadily Marnus Labuschagne reached his 50 off 145 balls which consisted of 3 boundaries and had taken the score to past 150. Australia was now getting into their comfort zone, Marnus understood that the pitch was getting better for batting and he could take his chances now.

Just after the tea break the pitch had now got better to bat and the conditions were now even better to bat, Marnus who had completed his 5o in 145 balls was now taking on the bowlers and was smashing boundaries at ease and was rotating the strike, Wade on the other hand had now started to play the role of second fiddle.

Marnus was now in his 90s and the partnership between them had already reached 100, Labuschagne played a beautiful cover drive to bring his century, the first of the series after missing out agonizingly in Sydney, and one of his best knocks in home conditions.

India was now under a lot of pressure a wicket or two from here could help India get back on track, and it was the debutant Natarajan who did the trick for India. Natarajan first took the wicket of Matthew Wade and then cleaned up Marnus Labuschagne who was dismissed for a well-made 108.

With around 20 more overs to left for the day's play, to end Cameron Green and Captain Tim Paine, took the team to safety by notching a good 50-run partnership.

Australia ended Day 1 at 274/5, The Indian bowlers especially Natarajan and Sundar had held their lines and bowled beautifully, with people thinking that this Indian team would be a pushover the Indians had done everything properly and nicely.

DAY 2

Tim Paine and Cameron Green began the day for Australia on Day 2, and it was T Natarajan who was extremely impressive on Day 1 to start the proceedings for India and Green on an extremely positive note by driving Natarajan twice in the very first over itself.

India had already seen the counter-attacking Green once in Sydney and they didn't want the Australian score to go past their reach and needed to break through the partnership as quickly as possible, and it was Shardul Thakur who was lovingly known as Lord Shardul who broke the dangerous-looking partnership and took the wicket of Tim Paine and then packed Pat Cummins in quick succession.

Sundar was brought to clean up Cameron Green and the spinner didn't disappoint anyone as he cleaned Wonderboy Green by a beauty, India had gotten back into the game big time, and the score which was looking to go over 450, was now being restricted to around 340-350.

The inexperienced Indian bowling had given a statement, they had given it back to the Australians, the bowling was extremely good, the line and length were followed and with Rahane's shrewd captaincy, the bowling changes were on point, and India was dominating the first session of Day 2.

A small partnership between Starc and Lyon propelled Australia to 369, a good score but the way things looked at the start of the innings and the game, India could give themselves a pat on the back with the way they bowled and the way the Indians showed the character, but the job was not yet done, 3 days were still to go in the test match, things were ought to be tight and the match could take a drastic change at any given time.

Natarajan, Shardul, and Sundar all took three wickets and showed that they were good bowlers and that the Indians have a good backup in the bowling department. In case there are any injuries in the future the backup is so well prepared that they would raise their hand and bowl extremely well.

The Indian team had three openers and they had to choose who would open the innings for India, with Rohit and Gill complementing each other extremely well in the Sydney test it was decided that both Sharma and Gill would open the innings for India, and Mayank Agarwal would slot in the middle order where he could use his experience to counter the second new ball. India had to be careful of any error or lapse in concentration that could give Australia a sniff would cause trouble for the Indians.

Sharma and Gill were extremely tentative in the first few overs, they knew that the ball would be moving a little and it would cause a fair amount of problems, bowlers with the ability of Starc and Hazlewood knew how to cause problems, and they were bowling in the right areas which was making it difficult for the Indian openers to play.

Taking advantage of the tentative batting by the Indians, Pat Cummins broke through Shubman Gill's defense and made him play a tentative shot which caught the edge of his bat and Steve Smith pouched a beautiful catch at second slip.

In came Pujara who was one of the heroes for India from that famous drawn test at Sydney, India was reliant on Pujara as they needed a good start and a partnership between him and Rohit Sharma was going to be vital for India's plans.

Rohit Sharma continued to play his shots and take on the bowlers he was pulling, driving, and cutting the Australians without any fear and knew that a good innings by him was the need of the hour. Rohit who was making his comeback in test cricket as an opener had a lot to prove to his critics and experts who doubted his ability as an opener in the longest format of the game.

Sharma who was looking good, but Rohit Sharma being Rohit Sharma looked to attack the spinner and holed out at long-on, he had once again thrown away his wicket, despite batting at a decent rate.

India was now 2 down for 60, and it was going to be important for Rahane and Pujara to bat till the end of the second session, and as decided with 6 overs of play remaining the two didn't score and were just defending and were looking to save their wicket. Rahane was trying to assess the pitch but decided to continue cautiously because a wicket here or there could have caused trouble for the Indians.

Tea was taken and the scoreboard read – India – 62 /2.

The weather was not very good, and the predictions suggested that it would rain during the later stages of day 2 and that is what happened the game for the day didn't happen any further and India closed the day at 62/2, with Pujara and Rahane remaining unbeaten for the day.

DAY 3

India was still 307 runs behind, and there was still a lot of work remaining, the onus was on the shoulders of Cheteshwar Pujara and Ajinkya Rahane and the middle order with Pant and Mayank Agarwal to follow.

Pujara and Rahane started cautiously and played to the merit of the ball, the Indians were rotating the strike, unlike the way they were batting towards the end of the day on Day 2.

Rahane had come out to bat with a positive intent and the way he batted only showed India's thinking and mindset that they wanted to reach the total and wanted to prove a point. The heartbreak of 36 at Adelaide was forgotten, everyone had brushed it aside. To India's advantage, only 3 players who had played that infamous test in Adelaide were playing in Brisbane. This meant that it was fresh blood for the Indians and what they knew was to win and defeat and torment the opposition by playing smart cricket.

Hazlewood and Starc were at the peak of their bowling, it was very beautiful seeing them ball they were attacking the batters by asking them the right questions and were not afraid of bowling bouncers or hitting the experienced Indian batters.

India needed to be careful a mistake here or there could have opened the gates and would have caused problems and then Australia would be eyeing a big first-innings lead.

Everyone thought that India had overcome the difficult phase of the innings but Hazlewood and Starc decided not to make the lives of Indian batters easy and got the wickets of Pujara, Rahane, Pant, and Agarwal.

India who were going good at 100/2 and had fought against Starc and Hazlewood had been struck with lightning. India was now suddenly 160/5 after the loss of Mayank Agarwal's wicket.

In came the debutant Washington Sundar to accompany Rishabh Pant, Sundar and Pant went a long way back as both the players played for India in the U19 Cricket World Cup in 2016 where the Indians had finished runners-up.

Sundar had a big task on hand, Sundar a more than capable batter needed to hang in and support Rishabh Pant. Washington Sundar who used to bat up the order in first-class cricket for Tamil Nadu was making his debut at number 7 for India, the two batters needed to bat well and had to bring the deficit down to as low as possible.

Rishabh Pant, on the other hand, was batting extremely well, without any pressure but with utmost responsibility, he was looking to just play out the bowlers with the strokes and unsettle them by hitting boundaries off their bowling in the same manner he did in the 2nd Innings of the Sydney test.

But a splendid catch by Cameron Green at gully had cut short, Pant's innings. India was now in all sorts of trouble as the scoreboard read India – 186/6. India were still 183 runs behind.

With tea still 20 overs away, Australia was thinking of bowling India out cheaply so they could get a substantial lead, and then play India out of the test match by giving them a huge fourth-innings target.

Shardul Thakur now joined Washington Sundar in the middle, it was a big task for the two Indian batters and now they had to do something special to get the lead down substantially. Shardul Thakur had a history with the bat, people who had followed him in his school days knew what he was capable of.

One such story is told to me about Shardul, by my friend and a brilliant cricket journalist Mr Suvajit Mustafi who once told me that Shardul had hit 6 sixes in an over in a School league in Mumbai.

And Shardul did the same, the first scoring shot by his bat was a six when he hooked Pat Cummins wide off fine leg. India was now trying to rebuild, this six from Shardul Thakur was a statement that India was not going down without a fight and they were going to score and attack the Australian bowling lineup.

Shardul didn't just stop here he was attacking Pat Cummins, he had decided that he would take the attack to the opposition, Shardul in the same over hit a beautiful four through mid-off, and trust me it felt like the spirit of Tendulkar, Richards, and Lara had gotten into him, the question was, how long would these guys continue, can they continue for a bit too longer, can the Indians bring down the lead down to 100.

Sundar on the other hand was taking his time, he was taking the singles and doubles and hitting the odd boundary, By the end of the drinks both had taken India's score past 200 and India was now 215/6.

The Australians knew this was a small resurgence by the Indians and they needed quick wickets to stop this mini resurgence otherwise it could become a great partnership and start an Indian juggernaut.

These two were looking comfortable, they were attacking and also playing with common sense, and without any problems, they were attacking the pacers and irritating the Australians by their defiance.

The two were not just showing how cricket needs to be played but they showed the world what the Indian spirit and Indians can do when they make their minds up. The faces of the Australian players showed that both Shardul and Sundar had started to irritate them.

Both had just one thing going on in their head, both had to play the entirety of the remaining second session and take India to safety. Just an over before tea India's score had reached 250, and India were looking extremely stable. India ended the session with a score of 243. Shardul was unbeaten on 33 and Sundar was unbeaten on 38.

Just after the tea break, the Australian captain was looking animated and was trying to motivate the players to make inroads into the Indian lineup and try to close the Innings at the earliest. Sundar and Shardul on the other hand were extremely confident of their batting skills and were looking to attack the Aussies with their attacking and defiant style of batting.

Shardul was attacking and smashing the Australian pace attack to pieces, he was driving the bowlers to all corners, it was so soothing to see the Indian lower order hang in and attack the opposition and it was also heartening to see the rate at which the Indians were scoring the runs and moving ahead.

Shardul was inching closer to his maiden half-century and Nathan Lyon came to the attack, Shardul stepped down the pitch got to the pitch off the ball, and heaved the ball over long-on to bring up a well-compiled 50. The Indians were ecstatic and Ashwin in his show had said that he had told Sridhar who was the fielding coach of the Indian team that Shardul would get to his fifty with a six and he proved his senior pro correct.

Slowly and steadily the partnership between Sundar and Shardul had now reached 100, and India was going very strong as the Australian target had now got down to less than 100.

Sundar was now reaching his half-century and he played a shot to mid-on and completed his half-century, it didn't feel like he was making his debut but it felt like he had already played 25-30 test matches. India was looking extremely good and the two young men had already made India proud.

Also, a piece of good news coming from the Indian camp was that Saini was ready to come out to bat. Shardul and Sundar had batted very beautifully, the two players had made the Indian fans extremely proud.

The way two batted, not only made everyone but I went overboard and said that if I ever had a son I would name him "Shardul Sundar."

I had told the same story to Washington Sundar when I met him in Bangalore during the finals of the Deodhar trophy, he had a smile on his face as I said one thing " Thank you for your innings at Brisbane, and I will name my son after you"

It was innings by both Sudar and Shardul one of the finest knocks, any cricket fans had seen.

Shardul's gritty knock had come to an end after Cummins cleaned him up with a beautiful ball that nipped back and did a little too much.

Sundar on the other hand had now taken the role of the aggressor and he might have played the shot of the series, as he hit a no-see six of Nathan Lyon over the cow corner. It was a beautiful shot and everyone commentating about the game had gotten off their seats just seeing the audacity by which Sundar had hit the six.

The last of the Indian tail wagged a little as Siraj smashed 2 boundaries and Natarajan faced thunderbolts from Hazlewood and Cummins. When he was asked about how he faced the balls he said he just kept his bat in the way and the ball found a way to hit the bat.

India was bundled out for 336, and Australia had a slender lead of 33, at one point when they were looking to be bowled out for 200, but the historic partnership between Shardul and Sundar took India closer to Australia's first innings total.

Australia came to bat in the second innings with 6 overs in hand and went on to add 21 more runs to the slender lead they had in the first innings with all the wickets intact. We were in for a brilliant finish to the test match, India brought the game back in the balance, with their defiance and brilliant performance.

DAY 4

After an exciting Day 3, Australia was ahead by just 50 runs, the World media started to talk about India's defiance in the test match now, the way they were locking horns with the Australians. The Indians were extremely proud of the way the team had played Shardul and Sundar had now become cult heroes, but the task was half done.

Indians needed to forget what they had done on Day 3 and now had to play with more strength to get a favorable result. India had a huge task on their hands, anything could have happened, if they let the foot off the gas. They needed to be accurate.

Warner and Harris came out to bat against the Indian pace quartet of Siraj, Shardul, Saini, and Natarajan. The good news coming from the Indian camp was that Saini could bowl a few overs if required as he was bowling in the nets before the start of the play and was not feeling a lot of strain near his groin region.

Warner and Harris started on a very positive note, they batted positively, and even though the Indian bowlers were extremely disciplined, they didn't let the bowlers take their wickets for free.

Both the openers slowly and steadily, attacking the bad balls and rotating the strike stitched a beautiful 50-run partnership, this was the first time in the test series that the Aussie openers had stitched a partnership of 50 runs or more.

The lead was growing and India needed to get a few quick wickets to put pressure back on the Aussies as the runs were coming thick and fast now. Indian Captain Ajinkya Rahane took the rabbit out of his hat and brought his trump card into the attack, Washington Sundar.

Sundar who had bowled in good lines and lengths during the first innings and had a dream run with the bat in his first test innings, needed to continue his good run in the test match, had to bowl well and break the partnership for India to restrict Australia to a realistic and chasable total.

The pressure that was applied by Sundar from one end was exploited and taken to India's advantage by Shardul Thakur, who was bowling in tandem with Sundar. A short ball directed into the body was swayed away by Harris and brushed past the gloves to go into the hands of Rishabh Pant.

The famous saying in cricket which says "One brings two", happened with the Aussies, as in the span of 6 balls both the openers were back in the hut and Australia was now reduced to 91/2.

Siraj was now brought into the attack after an initial spell of burst from Sundar and Shardul, it was high time that the Indians bowled in the right areas and got a few quick wickets to put pressure on the Australians. For India, it was important not to let Smith and Labuschagne settle as both of them were coming into this innings with a string of good scores.

Siraj made sure that both Labuschagne didn't stay on the crease for long and took the game away from India, India was now on top as Australia had lost 4 wickets for 123 runs.

India just needed to keep the pressure going and needed to attack more to get a wicket. Saini who had gotten injured during the first innings was also now bowling for India, good news was compiling for India and India was taking confidence from that.

Green had joined Smith in the middle and from the word go both were looking to play counter-attacking innings and were looking to induce frustration in the Indians. Both the batters were screaming No-runs, talking, and making faces, they were looking to unsettle the Indians. The best thing about this set of Indian players who were playing the game was that were calm and were not going to be shaken by small hiccups or sledging from the opposition.

Rahane and Pujara were the calmest people on the ground then, and they had passed on the message to the other younger teammates, that they needed to remain calm and not lose their patience at any point.

A small partnership was brewing between Smith and Green and both of them were playing Natarajan with ease, even though the bowler was putting pressure on the two batters, they were unmoved and were not giving away wickets or letting the Indian make headway.

Rahane once again went to his premier bowler, Siraj and once again Siraj didn't disappoint his captain as he took the big wicket of Steven Smith who was looking dangerous and was looking to take the game away from India, a well-directed short ball, which took a little part of the bat on its way to Rahane who had stationed himself at Gully.

Smith had reviewed the call thinking it had taken the glove as his hand had come off the handle. But the DRS, the players, and the on-field umpire had seen and understood the right thing. India was now on top and had gotten a huge wicket.

Now the task ahead of the Indian bowlers was to wrap the Australian innings at the earliest, and for this, Rahane summoned Shardul Thakur who took the wickets of Green, Tim Paine, and Nathan Lyon bowling short and into the deck.

Siraj and Shardul were bowling well in tandem and their performance was extremely good, both had taken 4 wickets a piece and both had an opportunity to get their first-ever 5-wicket haul in international cricket.

Fittingly it was Siraj who got his first-ever fifer and it came in the most dreamy fashion ever as a short ball was ramped by Hazlewood and was taken by Shardul Thakur at third man. India had wrapped up the Australian innings for 294, and now needed 328 to win a famous test and Brisbane, a place where Australia had not lost since 1988.

India's bowling performance made sure that India was not batted out of the test and it was also important to note that the new bowling lineup had taken 20 wickets in the test match.

A very beautiful moment was captured in the cameras, and which made a place in all the Indian fan's hearts was when Siraj was leading the Indian team into the pavilion after the innings where senior pro Jasprit Bumrah was seen hugging him and appreciating his performance in the absence of himself, Shami, Umesh and Ishant Sharma.

It was now onto the batters to get the job done, with rain looming around the corner, India needed to be careful and just play the day off and ensure that all the wickets remained intact.

To achieve a famous win at Gabba, India needed 328 to win in approximately 100 overs, in came the Indian openers Rohit Sharma and Shubman Gill.

Starc opened the bowling for Australia from one end and was welcomed by a beautiful shot through the off-side from Rohit Sharma. Hazlewood came into bowl the second over of the day and mid-way into the over, the rain picked up and the umpires called for the covers.

The day's play was called off as India ended the day with 4/0 on the scorecard. India had survived the tough part of the day's play and had survived without any damage or dent.

DAY 5

To win the famous test on the final day India needed 324 to win with 10 wickets in hand and 98 overs to decide the winner of the test series and Border-Gavaskar Trophy.

For India, it was an easy option to play out the draw and retain the Border-Gavaskar Trophy but for Australia, they had only one option and that was winning the game, there was no other option, winning was very important for Australia. The Australians hadn't won a Border-Gavaskar trophy since 2014-15, and playing out a draw was not going to give them their desired outcome.

In hindsight, India was looking to win their second consecutive test series on the bounce in Australia, which would have been a great achievement for India, given the number of injuries and number of players who made their debuts in the 4 match test series.

India had to be careful, they had to make sure that they played properly and not lose any wickets early, take the game as deep as possible, and maybe leave it on players like Rishabh Pant and Washington Sundar to finish the game.

It was a gloomy morning in Brisbane and it was going to swing a little, the two Indian openers needed to play out the new ball and wait for the ball to get old and the pitch to wear out a little so that scoring could be easy.

India's mindset was quite clear and it was understood in their body language that they had come to play the game with passion and had a positive mindset towards the game and with regards to the result of the game.

In came Rohit Sharma and Shubman Gill on the final day of this enthralling test series, a series which had seen everything, a historic low score, a great defiance, and a story of passion, resilience, and love.

Hazlewood was ready to bowl and complete his over, Gill left the ball as he started on a positive note for Australia with a little swing first up.

With the ball swinging and the pitch assisting the bowlers the two Indian openers didn't have much on offer and also didn't tease the ball and were just focusing on rotating the strike and getting the odd singles and doubles that were on offer, the weather was difficult to bat and the outfield was not supporting the Indian batters, India had to be more careful, the team knew a small opening and the Australian quicks and Nathan Lyon would pounce on them and finish the game.

The Aussie Captain Tim Paine was quick in his thinking and summoned his premier fast bowler Pat Cummins, and the plan was clear from Cummins as he was trying to make Rohit Sharma play on the front foot and get that outside edge which would carry to the keeper or first slip.

Cummins was continuously irritating both the openers and there was a lot of talking and chin music from the Australian bowlers and fielders the going was very tough and Cummins was bowling full throttle and garnering advantage from the conditions.

In the 9th Over Cummins, who was troubling Rohit continuously found the outside edge of his bat and Paine took a beautiful catch diving to his right towards the first slip and India lost their first wicket for 18. This is what India didn't want and this is what happened India was struggling to get the runs and now they had lost the wicket of their premier batter.

In came Australia's prime nemesis and India's sankatmochan (problem solver) Cheteshwar Pujara, the stage was set for Pujara, the ball was doing a bit too much and he had to stand there and just keep batting and batting. It was important that the two batters and any other batter who was going to come kept on batting and didn't lose his concentration.

India was calmly accumulating the runs, there was no sense of hurry, they knew they had time on their side, and chasing 3 runs per over wasn't a difficult task given the age and day the Indians were playing, the weather forecast had also forecasted the conditions to get better and with the sun shining bright it was going to be advantage batsmen and even if India needed 100 of the last 20 overs, with wickets in hand it was going to be T20 cricket all over again and with Mayank, Rishabh, and Washington Sundar in the middle order, India knew they have to preserve wickets and not take risks, the middle order and the lower middle order was capable enough to win the game for India.

Even though the conditions were tough, the application shown by both Gill and Pujara was commendable, they were not giving it away. Gill was being tempted in the same way as Rohit Sharma, but he was using his feet to perfect usage, and there was no slack from the young opener end.

While Shubman was continuing to attack, Cheteshwar Pujara was irritating and tiring the bowlers, with a typical Pujara show, the best thing about Cheteshwar Pujara was that he had understood his task, he knew the team needed him to step up and perform in a way that allows players like Shubman, Rishabh to play in a manner they like and which suited their style of play.

India was looking good, the team was performing in a good manner the runs had now started to come and they were coming at a good rate, Shubman was picking up speed and attacking Starc. The way Gill was attacking Mitchell Starc, it didn't feel like a young player was playing, it felt as if an experienced batter was giving his all.

Shubman had reached his 50 off just 90 balls, and it was the start of something very special, Gill was not shying away from attacking the bowlers, he was attacking and smashing them all around the corner. Gill's aggression after lunch had given India not only hope but an edge in the game.

The best part of this period of play was the way Shubman had attacked Mitchell Starc, a bowler of Starc's stature was being hit all over the park and it was extremely beautiful to watch, the shots were predominantly of the backfoot, and the shots were mesmerizing and the fans were in awe of Shubman's talent.

To counter Shuban Gill's innings, Tim Paine brought the experienced Nathan Lyon, to the attack, who was bowling from over the wicket to attack the stumps and get Gill forward, so that the ball catches the outside edge and the batter gets caught at Slips. Lyon was continuously bowling on that line and length and was troubling the Indian batter, he kept on bowling the same thing and was successful as one oddball took the edge of Gill's bat and the catch was neatly taken by Steven Smith.

Shubman Gill had played a fantastic knock and scored a brilliant 91, he missed out on a fantastic hundred and made sure that the Australians didn't make an early inroad after getting Rohit Sharma's wicket.

India was now 132/2 after the fall of Gill's wicket and India now needed less than 200 runs and had 8 wickets in hand. Ajinkya Rahane came in with proper intent, he didn't look at the bowler and started smashing both Hazlewood and Lyon. India very well knew that this was a moving session and if they played positively in this session, they could get a positive result out of this test match.

Both Shubman Gill and Ajinkya Rahane did a fantastic job by counter-attacking the Australian bowlers and on the other hand, Cheteshwar Pujara irritated the bowlers by just taking singles and playing dots, but it was not easy to be Cheteshwar Pujara at that particular moment as the bowlers were panicking and getting irritated, They were now attacking Pujara with short balls and instead of bowling stump line were attacking his body and giving him body blows.

The experienced Indian campaigner knew what he was up with and took the blows and didn't lose concentration, the resilience shown by Pujara was irritating and weakening the Australian team, which meant that Rahane could take advantage of it and was attacking the bowling.

Rahane was continuously attacking Lyon and Hazlewood, he didn't wait for anything and he knew that once he took charge and attacked the Australians, the flow of runs would help India settle their nerves and bring panic in the Aussie dugout.

Cummins was brought into the attack just to break the brewing partnership, and he eventually got the wicket of Ajinkya Rahane, who played a counter-attacking 24 off just 22 balls. India was now 167/3, and guess who came to bat!! It was the hero from Sydney, RISHABH PANT. Pant had a big task on hand he knew what wasn't achieved in Sydney had to be done in Gabba, he knew what was on stake and how he had to get the job done, the game had now come into Rishabh's territory, attack, attack and win!

With Rishabh Pant, in and India still needing half of the runs to win this test match, it was now a case of who loses the patience first, the Australian bowlers or the Indian batters, the biggest advantage for India was Rishabh and Pujara batting together and Mayank yet to come, who could face the second new ball if required. India needed to be composed they had all the time in the world to score the runs and get the win, the Indian players needed to be careful, rest would be taken care of given how Rishabh and Pujara complimented each other.

Tea was taken and India was now 183/3, India needed 125 in the last session to win the historic test match in Gabba, the adrenaline was high in all supporters, and the feeling of achieving a great series win was on the cusp. Defeating once an invincible team in their home was now looking possible for the Indian team.

India now needed to be patient and treat this game as an ODI, and try to make the game into a t20 where they would need 5 runs per over or 6 runs per over in the last 10 to 14 overs.

The first half an hour was going to be crucial and India pounced on the opportunity. The Australians tried to up the pace of the game by introducing Marnus Labuschagne into the attack by his captain who was cut by Cheteshwar Pujara to bring up his half-century.

Pujara's fifty came in 196 balls, his slowest half-century but one of his most important half-centuries. India was looking in full control and the commitment from the Indian batters was seen in abundance. The Australian captain tried intimidating Rishabh Pant who is known to be excellent against spinners and likes to take on them.

Lyon was continuously bowling a tempting line, with long on and a short third man, to get the wicket of Rishabh Pant. A chance had come Australia's way but the captain Tim Paine couldn't make the best of the opportunity.

Rishabh had danced down the pitch to hit the ball over long on for maximum but missed the ball completely, Tim Paine was also not able to gather the ball and the ball went past the keeper and Steve Smith who was stationed at slips.

Rishabh was playing very carefully, he had understood that it was important for him to stay till the end and India played in that particular manner, where they took their time, and took the game into a place where the game became a T20 game.

The new ball was taken at the 80-over mark and it had started to drizzle a little bit, but the skies were clear so there was no option to stop the game. Tim Paine immediately called his premium fast bowler Pat Cummins to bowl with the new ball as he understood that this was Australia's last chance to get a wicket and create an issue for India.

With the new ball came the wicket of Cheteshwar Pujara, Pujara was given LBW by the on-field umpire, which a lot of people thought was going over the stumps and the same doubt was there in the mind of Pujara and he reviewed the decision, but to everyone's disappointment the ball tracking showed the ball was going clipping the stumps and it was an umpire call, which meant that the decision would be upheld and Pujara had to go back for well compiled 56. He had received many body blows but his concentration was not breakable.

In came Mayank Agarwal, who knew how to face the new ball being an opener. But, the Bangalore lad had a task on his hand, the conditions were a little difficult and the ball was swinging way too much.

India needed only 100 to win the test match and had as many 20 overs in hand, 5 runs per over was the task. The key for India was going to be Rishabh Pant, the longer Rishabh stayed the better result India was about to get. One of the two batters needed to bat till the end for India to reach the target and win the match and the series.

The world had no idea in which direction the game was going, the game was in for a photo finish and every Indian fan had their hearts in their mouth.

Agarwal and Rishabh Pant started to accumulate the runs and played according to the situation. Rishabh Pant had scored a brilliant 50 off 100 balls and knew it was important for the Wicket-keeper to stay and bat till the end.

India was now on the move and the runs were coming thick and fast. In between Pujara's dismissal and Drinks, 28 balls were bowled, and a total of 31 runs was scored. India were now 259/4. India now needed 69 runs to win in 15 overs, on the other hand, Australia needed wickets.

Pat Cummins was bowling on the trot and was looking to take a wicket, he had already taken the wicket of Cheteshwar Pujara in this spell and was looking to take another, Mayank who was batting at 9 received a peach of a delivery, which went past the outside edge through to the keeper, there was a massive appeal, which was turned down by the umpire but the Australians decided to review as the few senior men thought it had taken the edge, the snicko didn't show any murmur and the umpire's decision was upheld.

But, the very next ball, Agarwal was caught by Wade at short cover. Mayank Agarwal was dismissed for 9 and India were now 265/5 and needed another 63 to win.

In came the hero of the first innings, Washington Sundar this time to make a partnership with his U19 partner Rishabh Pant.

Rishabh Pant, being there was giving India the confidence to be happy, slowly and steadily the two were compiling the runs, they were taking their time, not taking risks, rotating the strike.

Washington had decided to attack Cummins who was bowling a long spell and, on the trot, Sundar had decided there was a need to attack the bowler and get the run rate a little down, Cummins was successful in doing that Sundar first hooked Cummins for a six and later hit a boundary past the slip cordon which brought down the target to less than 40.

Seeing this Rishabh changed his gear and in the very next over smashed Lyon for two consecutive boundaries and the fairytale was being lived. I was very young to remember what happened in Kolkata 2001, but I was old enough to understand what was going on in Gabba, with every ball and every run scored I felt happy, there were cheers, shouting, abusing the Australians, and the world who had counted India down and out after the loss and debacle as we say in Adelaide.

Suddenly Australia was feeling the heat and they had started to make mistakes, Tim Paine again was leaving the balls and was not able to lead his team properly. India was now getting close to the target and had breached 300.

Things were getting special, with every passing run India was getting close to the target, Indians in the crowd were jumping, and the members of the Bharat Army on the ground were witnessing something special, we on our television sets were witnessing something beautiful.

I had a quiz that was going on and trust me I had just turned on the laptop and didn't care to give the quiz, just selected random options and gave the answers.

With 10 required, Sundar played a shot that was not required and got himself bowled, but the best thing was India now only needed 10 to win.

Rishabh smashed a four off Hazlewood and India was a hit away, Rishabh Pant was riding his luck and was taking India home, with 6 to get, Rishabh Pant had thought of the commentary which would be said about him as he smashed a six over mid-wicket, but to his bad luck when he tried smashing Hazlewood the ball took the top edge and dropped in the no man's land.

Now Shardul thought he could be the hero and be the hero for India, but this time he lobbed it in the air and Lyon at square leg pouched an easy catch. It is also said that Rohit was so angry at Shardul that he had planned to give an earful to Shardul but was stopped by Ajinkya Rahane who told him, let us win the game, we will deal with him after that.

Thanks to the presence of mind from Shardul and Rishabh both had crossed each other and Rishabh was on strike.

India now needed 3, it was the last ball of Hazlewood's over it was angling across to off-stump and as Rishabh hit the ball it went past the fielder at extra cover, as it went past the fielder I thought at least we would now get two but as the ball kept rolling on the green grass of Gabba, it had one thing written that India was going to breach Gabba, and as the ball touched the boundary line, there was an elation of emotions.

India had breached Gabba, India had won the game, India had won the series, India had buried the ghosts of COVID-19, 36 at Adelaide, and whatnot. Everyone in the team knew they wouldn't play together again, so they decided to make history with the one elusive opportunity they had.

There was running, hugging emotions, tears of happiness, and a great series had come to an end. India had won, they had played out of their skins, and they didn't have Virat Kohli, Jasprit Bumrah, Mohammed Shami, Umesh Yadav, Ravi Jadeja, Ravi Ashwin, Hanuma Vihari and Ishant Sharma, but with a new India they won the series, they won the hearts and souls of every cricket lover in the world.

Rishabh Pant, Shardul, Sundar, Natarajan, Siraj all had become a country-wide sensation. Tim Paine who had asked Ashwin to come to Gabba, here were the Indians, who had broken the Aussie arrogance of being unbeaten at Gabba.

This victory is remembered as one of India's greatest test wins, a win that tested the character, mindset, and passion of all the cricketers in the team.

India had won the series 2-1 and retained the Border-Gavaskar Trophy.

But as fans and as supporters the best part of the win according to me was the celebration of the win was extremely memorable, my friends Goutam, Rishabh, and Varad had spammed "Gabba Is Breached" during our class in the Webex meeting and the professor named me Gabba to commemorate this big win.

The win acted as a healing agent on the wound after what was going on in the country the way COVID was attacking everyone and the terror it had caused.

This victory is etched in the memories of every cricket fanatic. To the energy of the victory at Gabba, To the Energy of Young India.

And as Shakespeare says, "All is well, that End's Well". It was indeed a happy ending for the Indian cricket team.

THE END

www.ingramcontent.com/pod-product-compliance
Lightning Source LLC
LaVergne TN
LVHW091103150826
845673LV00002B/700
9798892334754